How to be a Motivational Manager

Some other titles from How To Books

Psychometric Tests for Graduates
*Gain the confidence you need to excel at graduate-level
psychometric and management tests*

Practice Psychometric Tests
*How to familiarise yourself with genuine recruitment tests and get
the job you want*

Management Level Psychometric & Assessment Tests
Everything you need to help you land that senior job

How to be Headhunted
The insiders guide to making executive search work for you

How to Write a Great CV
Prepare a powerful CV that really works

howtobooks

How To Books Ltd
Spring Hill House
Spring Hill Road
Begbroke, Oxford OX5 1RX
email: info@howtobooks.co.uk
www.howtobooks.co.uk

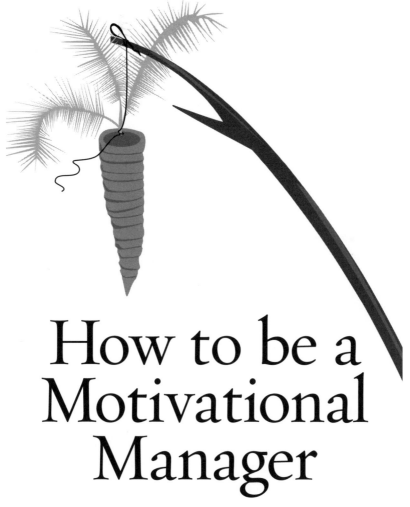

How to be a
Motivational
Manager

AN ESSENTIAL GUIDE FOR LEADERS
AND MANAGERS WHO NEED TO GET FAST
RESULTS WITH MINIMUM STRESS

Alan Fairweather

howtobooks

Published by How To Books Ltd
Spring Hill House
Spring Hill Road
Begbroke, Oxford OX5 1RX
Tel: (01865) 375794. Fax: (01865) 379162
email: info@howtobooks.co.uk
www.howtobooks.co.uk

How To Books greatly reduce the carbon footprint of their books
by sourcing their typesetting and printing in the UK.

© 2007 Alan Fairweather
First edition 2007
Reprinted 2008

British Library Cataloguing in Publication Data
A catalogue record for this book is available from the British
Library

ISBN 978 1 84528 225 7

Cover design by Baseline Arts Ltd, Oxford
Produced for How to Books by Deer Park Productions, Tavistock
Typeset by Pantek Arts Ltd, Maidstone, Kent
Printed and bound by Cromwell Press Ltd, Trowbridge, Wiltshire

NOTE: The material contained in this book is set out in good
faith for general guidance and no liability can be accepted
for loss or expense incurred as a result of relying in particular
circumstances on statements made in this book. Laws and
regulations are complex and liable to change, and readers should
check the current position with the relevant authorities before
making personal arrangements.

Contents

1
Tough enough to care

IS THIS WHAT YOU CALL FEEDBACK?

'You little b*****d. What kind of job do you call this? You've made a complete f*****g mess of these clips. Get them fixed you useless little b*****d and I need them today!'

These were some of the first words I heard on the first day of my working life. I'm glad to say they weren't directed at me personally but at one of my hapless fellow apprentices in the training department of a Glasgow engineering factory. The person handing out the verbal abuse was our beloved supervisor, Tommy.

Of course, Tommy wouldn't regard his tirade as verbal abuse, it was just the way he communicated his instructions to us when he was unhappy. Come to think of it, he communicated the same way when he *was* happy.

In my eyes, Tommy had replaced my schoolteacher as the person who kept me right, told me what to do and was responsible for my engineering education.

I went home on that first day near to tears and desperately regretting the lack of study that would have taken me on to university or college. However, college or not, I would still have to face, at some time in my life, the world of work and the people who would manage and supervise me. Maybe not every supervisor would be like Tommy; sad to say, many were.

So what did you learn today?

I spent five years in that engineering factory completing my apprenticeship and one year plotting my escape. It would be wrong to say I hated the place as there was a sort of natural acceptance that this was something I had to do, it was 'my work'.

However, it's also fair to say that I didn't learn much about engineering during these years. If you placed me anywhere near a lathe or a milling machine tomorrow I'd probably end up removing parts of my body.

Tommy's first instruction to me on day one was 'Goanmakyerselahama'. This was translated for me by one of my fellow apprentices as 'Go and find someone to show you how to make a hammer.' Excuse me! No blueprint to work to, no instruction and any chance of positive feedback on my progress? Somehow I don't think so; it was just a matter of get on with it, and if it wasn't right – 'I'll tell you about it.' Some of my fellow apprentices spent their first six months trying to make a hammer working mainly by trial and error; and as you'll probably have gathered, there was a lot of trial and error.

You need a 'y' to get on around here

During my five years I was moved around several departments to experience all aspects of mechanical engineering. I met several supervisors who all seemed to have a name like Tommy or Davy or Bobby. It appeared you had to have a name ending in 'y' to get promoted in this company. I was therefore pleased when an apprentice called Scud nicknamed me Stormy. If you want to know how that came about, check out my surname.

I remember one supervisor called 'Davy' who would arrive in the inspection department where I worked every morning dead on seven minutes past eight and then stride the length of the department. He walked up the middle between the benches where we slaved, swivelling his head from side to side and saying, 'Good morning – good morning – good morning.' He'd then disappear into his tiny cubicle and we'd never see him again all day. I suppose in his eyes he saw himself as a great communicator and a real people person. On the odd occasion that I entered his cubicle he would eye me up and down and then ask me what part of the factory I worked in. I took pains to explain that I was one of his devoted team.

In the inspection department I was assigned to work with a more experienced engineer and he told me what to do. Who told *him* what to do, I haven't a clue. I think Davy just communicated his instructions by telepathy. Oh, and by the way, this more experienced engineer I worked with was called Charley; he was obviously on his way up.

We really don't want to leave

I had a spell in the fitting-out workshop where we assembled components for submarine periscopes. They assigned me to another experienced engineer called John. Obviously his promotion prospects were limited until he got a 'y' on the end of his name. John was a real 'yes sir, no sir' type of guy. He did what he was told, kept his head down and got on with the job. I can remember him saying to me one day, 'Watch it son, here comes the boss, keep your head down and look busy.' At that point a senior manager would pass through the workshop in his three-piece suit, casting his eye over us servile peasants. It struck me even at that young age that there was something not quite right about this.

On the stroke of 4.30 in the afternoon the bell would ring, they'd open the gates and the factory would empty in thirty seconds. And woe betide you if you didn't run – you'd probably be crushed in the rush for freedom. There were a handful of disabled people who worked in this factory and they were allowed to leave ten minutes before the rest of us in case they were trampled by the able-bodied.

People in this environment only did what they were told to do and no more. They reluctantly trundled into work each morning, did their job and got out as quickly as they could at night.

Having fun certainly wasn't on the agenda so people looked to lighten up their day any way they could. I used to slip off to the men's room as often as I could to read my latest edition of Mickey Spillane.

Some people even resorted to causing trouble or some form of sabotage just for a laugh. One day I inadvertently wrecked a large lathe I was working on. We were all on a bonus system based on the number of components we could turn out in a given period. This meant getting the component to be machined into the lathe as quickly as possible, machining it and getting it out again. I was in the habit of slipping the fast-forward lever into reverse so as to bring the lathe to a halt almost immediately. This was standard practice for us all, but for me this day it all went wrong. The gearbox exploded with an almighty bang and I was left trying to explain what happened. This of course gave me a great deal of credibility with a certain section of my workmates as they thought I'd done it on purpose. That must have cost the company a great deal of money.

> *From what I could see, a manager or supervisor told you what to do and occasionally checked to see if you were doing it right.*

These five years were my introduction to work and managers, my initial programming as to what management was all about. From what I could see, a manager or supervisor told you what to do and occasionally checked to see if you were doing it right. They never told you *how* to do it right and they reprimanded you when you got it wrong.

They gave the impression that managing was all about dealing with people who didn't want to work, who wanted to do as little as possible and who would cause trouble whenever they had the chance.

These managers weren't bad people; they just managed the way they thought best, which was probably very similar to the way they were treated by *their* manager.

Maybe sales managers will be better

A sales job was what I wanted: master of my own destiny – smart suit – company car – expense account – clean hands. I was delighted to be out of that engineering factory and starting a much better job as a sales representative. A bit of me thought it would be much different as far as managers were concerned. I was leaving an engineering factory to work in a more business type of environment; surely the managers would be more sophisticated and hopefully friendlier?

However, for me it was pretty much more of the same. 'I'm the boss, I tell you what to do and if you don't do it right you're in trouble.'

> *'I'm the boss, I tell you what to do and if you don't do it right you're in trouble.'*

If you've ever worked in sales then I'm sure that you've experienced the 'macho' style that is prevalent in many organisations: 'Get out and get the order and don't let anyone stand in your way.'

I had three successful years in my first sales job selling electrical appliances into department stores. My manager there was a bit of a softy and gave me an easy time. He wasn't the kind of manager who was comfortable giving feedback whether it was good news or not so good. This meant that I was never sure if I was doing it right or if I could be doing it better. So, as with the engineering apprenticeship, I just learned the selling business as I went along.

How not to do it

In an attempt to further my sales career and use my engineering background, I joined a company in the welding consumables field. My job was to visit maintenance engineers in their workshops, demonstrate welding equipment, get the order and try not to set myself on fire. I passed through the initial four-week training course with flying colours and was assigned to work for an area supervisor called Peter. I learned so much from Peter, mainly how *not* to supervise people. I can remember thinking at the time, 'When I become a manager or a supervisor, I will never treat anyone the way Peter treats me.'

Peter demanded that I phone him every evening with details of how many customers I'd seen, how many demonstrations I'd done and how many orders I'd taken. The results I reported were never good enough and the successes were never recognised. How I hated him and his stupid toupee. I used to dread the evening telephone calls and I left home every morning feeling a huge pressure to perform better; quite naturally, this didn't help me sell any better.

Some days Peter would make calls with me on customers and afterwards, in the car, he would tell me all the things I'd done wrong.

As you'd probably expect, I hated this job and spent most of my time plotting how to push Peter under a bus and how to get a new job. It also had the effect of seriously undermining my confidence. Although I'd been in sales for four years, I was starting to think that perhaps I wasn't good enough and maybe it wasn't for me.

I was eventually accepted for a new sales job and I remember vividly the joy of writing my letter of resignation.

The next day I was summoned to a meeting with John the area manager, Peter's boss. 'Why are you leaving Alan? You're doing so well, we don't want you to go and you have a great future here.' You could have knocked me down with a feather. I'd been under the impression that I'd probably be sacked pretty soon for being so useless. Of course, as you'll realise, I wasn't useless, it was just another case of bad management.

I went on to be successful in other sales companies and was eventually promoted into an area manager's role. However, in my sales career I reported to many senior managers, many of whom didn't get the best out of me.

Is it better now?

You're probably thinking that I'm painting a very black picture and perhaps your experience of managers is much better than mine. You may also feel that we've come a long way since the days that I describe and that managers are much better now. And anyway, let's face it, they wouldn't get away with as much nowadays. However, many senior managers today are in my age group and were brought up in similar work environments to my own. This means that they've received the same 'programs' about how to manage people.

I believe managers nowadays are better but by no means good enough.

> *I believe managers nowadays are better but by no means good enough.*

I continually hear stories from friends and other contacts about how they're managed and it doesn't make good listening.

My friend Martin, who works for a US software company, was telling me recently about his Vice President of Sales. Apparently, this VP likes to run a question-and-answer session at his sales meetings. He has $1, $5 and $10 questions that he fires at his team and if you get the question right you win the money. Woe betide you if you get the question wrong. You're then humiliated in front of the team and you end up owing the VP the money. The VP obviously thinks that putting his team under pressure is a lot of fun and a good way for them to learn. So I asked Martin what he and his colleagues thought about this. 'I'm used to it', he said. 'I've been around a long time and I've been through this stuff before. However, the VP's overall way of running things and his "macho" style is starting to have a negative effect on the team. In fact, I'm starting to look for another job.'

How much does it cost the organisation?

People will often tell me about hard-driving managers they've known who ride roughshod over every one of their team but always achieve their target. The suggestion is that these managers must be successful because they achieve their business targets.

I've worked for managers like that; however, I'm also very much aware of the high turnover of people that those managers have to deal with. These managers are leading people who spend their evenings and weekends applying for new jobs. The team members are also not giving of their best when they're at work. As a result the manager has to drive them harder to stay on top of them. It's a vicious circle.

These managers also spend too much of their time and the company's money interviewing and recruiting new people.

In the first week of my sales job with the welding company I described earlier I was constantly hearing from the customers, 'Not another new salesman from your company.' They would then tell me how the salesman I was replacing had 'bad mouthed' the company and the managers before he left.

That organisation was relatively successful, but how much more successful could it have been with a happy and stable team? And think how easy its managers made it for their competitors to steal their business.

So much of what we call management consists in making it difficult for people to work.

Peter F. Drucker (1909–, American-Austrian management consultant)

THE FACTS SPEAK FOR THEMSELVES

For the past fourteen years I've been running seminars for staff and managers across a whole range of organisations and businesses. There's a lot of discussion going on in these seminars and I constantly hear complaints from staff about their managers and the organisations they work for.

When I run seminars for managers, many of them complain about their team, about the manager above them and, again, the organisation they work for.

It doesn't matter whether I'm working with a multinational organisation or a small company, the complaints are much the same.

The *Gallup Management Journal* conducted a survey among US workers aged eighteen or older and I quote from its report:

> 24.7 million, or 19%, are what we call actively disengaged. This term describes people who not only fail to be enthralled by their work but are fundamentally disconnected from it. Actively disengaged workers tend to be less productive and report being less loyal to their companies, more stressed and less secure in their work. They miss more days and are less satisfied with their personal lives.

In its research the Gallup organisation also discovered that 70 per cent of people don't leave their job – they leave their manager.

In its research the Gallup organisation also discovered that 70 per cent of people don't leave their job – they leave their manager.

The Society for Human Resource Management reports that in terms of productivity, the United States is performing at 62 per cent capacity. It also reports that the cost of paid unscheduled absenteeism rose sharply in 2002 to $755 per employee. Employers have stated that they earmark 5.1 per cent of a company's budget to pay for unscheduled absenteeism.

In the UK research by the Confederation of British Industry suggests that workplace absence is on the rise for the first time in five years. In 2006 we were off sick on average for 7.2 days, up from 6.8 the previous year. It costs UK businesses £11.75 billion a year. The CBI also estimates that 15% of all illness is due to people taking days off when they are not really ill.

A recent report in the *Gallup Management Journal* estimates that disengaged employees in Singapore are costing the country $4.9 billion annually, the root of disengagement being blamed on poor management.

So a lot of people are unhappy at work and therefore they tend to:

- Take more days off (one in three staff 'sick days' are not due to illness);

- Spend a lot of time looking for other jobs;

- Create internal problems;

- Lose sales;

- Let customers down.

There is too much evidence to suggest that managers are still not doing a good enough job with their people. The ironic thing is that the middle manager is the one who suffers most from unhappy staff.

I'm on your side

Now I know you're thinking about that figure of 70 per cent quoted above as the people who leave their manager and about the people who've left your team. You're likely thinking, 'The ones who left my team are probably in the 30 per cent and I'm doing my best as a manager.' However, you also have to ask yourself if you're suffering from any of the other factors listed above.

I know from speaking to managers that a great deal of their time is spent dealing with issues that are a result of staff absence, having to recruit new people and deal with staff and customer complaints.

You may also be feeling that I'm having a real go at you, but I believe we all have to bite the bullet sometimes for our own good. I believe many managers are making life hard for themselves mainly because they don't know how else to manage their people. They are also giving themselves a great deal of stress.

I know this because I've been there, I've made the mistakes and I've got the T-shirt. In my close contact with managers in various organisations I still see them making mistakes and conducting themselves in a way that makes their job harder.

Middle managers and supervisors are the most important people in any organisation. You're the person who has to get the best out of your team every day. However, your team's performance is determined by the relationship they have with you. I did the job of a manager for fifteen years and I know what's involved. You're the one stuck in the middle between the team member and your manager and that can be a hard sandwich to digest.

The way you treat your staff is the way they'll treat your customers.

Karl Albrecht

We're going on to look at what the successful managers do and what you can do to get even better and make your life a lot easier.

I've been talking about managers and supervisors up until now but I believe we need to think about ourselves more as Team Leaders. It doesn't matter whether you're in sales or customer service or in a production situation, you're responsible for a team of people and you're expected to achieve results through them.

However, for the purposes of this book I'm going to continue to use the word manager. I'm also going to switch genders all the time so that I'm not accused of being sexist.

So before we go on to look at how we get better, let's consider what we're up against.

WHY DON'T WE DO IT WELL?

The majority of managers that I've worked for and with were mediocre. Some of them were very poor and only one or two could be described as good. This isn't a personal attack on these people, it's just what I've experienced as a team member and colleague of these people. If you look back over your career then I'm sure you've had similar experiences. We're going to take a look at the good guys in a short while but for the moment let's consider why there are so many poor and mediocre managers. I believe that there are four reasons:

1. Because it's such a difficult job.

2. Nobody shows you what to do or gives you the right training.

3. The media and our culture send the wrong message.

4. Some people don't have what it takes to be a manager.

Why is it so difficult?

Managing, supervising, being a Team Leader is the hardest job in the world and I'll tell you why.

> *Managing, supervising, being a Team Leader is the hardest job in the world.*

Imagine what it's like to drive a car. You turn the key to start the engine, select drive or the gear you want and press the accelerator. The car then moves off. If you want to turn you rotate the steering wheel to the right or left, and to stop you press the brake pedal. All this was quite difficult when you first learned to drive but its easy now. If I asked you to drive my car, you might take a short while to get used to it, but you'd immediately be able to drive down to the supermarket and get me some food.

However, if I was to tell you that my car was different from any other you'd driven then I'm sure you'd have a problem. 'You don't start it with a key, there's a little switch somewhere. When you engage forward gear it might go backwards and if you turn the wheel left it might go right but sometimes it goes left. And the accelerator is what stops it and the brake pedal makes it go faster but not every day. You'll get used to it in time; I've lived with it for years.'

Managing people is pretty much like this. Every model is different and you need different skills to 'drive' each one. Just because pressing the gas pedal on one model makes it go forwards, doesn't mean to say that the next one will be the same; it might, but it might not.

The problem arises because we 'learn' on certain models and then find to our annoyance that the others are different. 'Why can't they all be the same?' we scream in frustration.

Human beings are the most complex and complicated pieces of 'equipment' you'll ever have to deal with. Many of them have similarities but every one of them is different and

> *Human beings are the most complex and complicated pieces of 'equipment' you'll ever have to deal with.*

they all work in a slightly different way. Your job as a manager is to get these complex humans working as efficiently as possible, but there's no one around to show you what to do and there's no instruction manual.

What also complicates the relationship between the manager and the team is this – human beings are driven totally by their emotions. We all make decisions based on our emotions and then try to justify our decision logically. Let me give you an example of what I mean. If you were to ask a friend why they'd bought an expensive Mercedes they would probably tell you it was because of the superb German engineering. They might also tell you that the decision was based on the high resale value. Well let me tell you now, it was none of these things – they bought the Mercedes to impress you and the neighbours. Their decision to buy that car is based solely on their emotions.

What's logic got to do with it?

When managers face a problem with one of their team they try to solve it logically and then they wonder why it all goes wrong.

Imagine that one of your team announces, 'I'm leaving this job. I've found another job doing the same thing and it pays more money.' You realise that you don't want to lose this team member so you approach your boss and agree an increase in salary. However, when you offer the increase in salary the team member turns you down. So you think logically, 'What's wrong with this person? Why are they leaving?'

They might be telling you that they're leaving for more money. However, that now doesn't seem to be the reason. It might be that they're leaving because they feel you just don't care about them.

I've seen this happen so often with the good guys in a team. Because they're one of the high achievers who don't give the manager any problem they get left alone too much. What happens then is they feel that the manager doesn't care about them so they leave.

Managing people is a hugely difficult job. A degree in psychology would help but if you haven't got that then stay with me – I've got the answers.

Trust me – I'm a manager

The second reason I gave you for poor managers relates to being shown what to do. Imagine the following scenario. You pay a visit to your doctor one day and in the course of the conversation he lets it slip that he has no formal medical qualification. However, everything's okay because he's been involved in the 'doctoring' business for years, had lots of experience and has read several books on the subject. I bet you'd be out of there like a shot.

Imagine another situation where you're looking to employ an auto mechanic to look after your company vehicles. One applicant tells you how good they are at fixing cars and trucks. They been doing it for years – the only thing is that they haven't served an apprenticeship or had any other formal training. Would you give them the job? Of course you wouldn't.

So why do so many organisations trust their most important and most expensive asset, their employees, to someone who has had no training in how to deal with people?

People most often get promoted into a manager's job because they know the business they're in and they know the products and the industry. Sometimes they also get promoted because they get on with the team and, ironically, in some cases because they don't. (Some senior managers believe that you shouldn't promote someone who is too 'close' to the team.)

When appointing a manager, organisations traditionally look for someone who can do all the 'management' things. All the technical skills required to do the job such as planning, cost control, resource allocation, interviewing, solving problems and dealing with customers.

Management training in many organisations usually addresses the activities listed above. Managers go on courses for time management, report writing and health and safety issues, among others. However, none of these activities helps the manager to motivate their team.

Before you start writing to me I'm aware that some organisations are running courses on leadership skills and management of change; more 'people skills' type of programmes. I know this because I'm running some of these courses. However, I also know that the people who come on my courses are often hearing for the first time about how to motivate their people. Some of them have been managers for over twenty years and have never had any people skills training.

> *It's often just taken for granted by senior managers in an organisation that managers will have the 'natural' skills to motivate, coach, give feedback and get the best out of their people.*

It's often just taken for granted by senior managers in an organisation that managers will have the 'natural' skills to motivate, coach, give feedback and get the best out of their people. Tiger Woods has the natural skill to play golf but he's been listening to trainers and coaches for years and he still does.

I didn't get any training when I started as a manager. I was left to get on with it and find out how to motivate my team. It worked out okay for the first few years but it was only when I started formal studies in motivation techniques at the Open University in the UK that my management success really took off. I've been reading books and studying successful managers for twenty-five years. That's why I've written this book and I know it will help you.

This book is going to show how to develop your skills, and also show you how to 'train' your manager.

It must be true, I saw it on TV

My third reason for poor managers blames the media and our culture for sending the wrong messages.

We've all heard the old cliché 'nice guys don't finish first', and that has a huge impact on how managers deal with their people. We're led to believe that successful managers are tough, courageous, 'no nonsense' people. And if you're weak or soft with your team, then you'll get walked on and taken advantage of.

A manager will often look at 'successful' managers in business or sport to try to understand what makes them successful. The media often portrays these people as tough guys who drive their people by the force of their personality, shouts and threats – no wimps allowed.

As I write, the UK edition of the television show, *The Apprentice*, has just started a new series on BBC Two. The US edition is about to start another season on NBC. In case you haven't seen it, it's the show that pits the hungriest business brains against each other to see which one is worthy of a six-figure salary and the chance to become Sir Alan Sugar's 'apprentice'. In the US, Donald Trump is the man the contestants have to impress.

Both of these high-flying self-made billionaires are portrayed as tough, no-nonsense individuals. Their catch phrase is 'Your Fired!'

Jack Welch, the ex-CEO of General Electric, writes in his book *Jack*:

> Strong managers who make tough decisions to cut jobs provide the only true job security in today's world. Weak managers are the problem. Weak managers destroy jobs.

That statement may be true. However, it leads managers to believe that they most certainly have to be 'strong'. There's no way that a manager wants to be perceived as weak. However, it's how you define 'tough' and 'strong' that decides how successful a manager you'll be.

We're all aware of the big tough sports coaches who run successful teams. In the United States the legendary Red Wings coach Scotty Bowman, often billed as the greatest coach in ice hockey, was well known as a relentless, heartless and humourless task master.

Another legend, American football coach Vince Lombardi, was known to work his teams hard. He pushed his players and made them repeat plays over and over till they got it right. He yelled at his teams for any mistakes, even after games they had won. He had rigid rules, imposed discipline and had no tolerance for mistakes. One of his famous lines is: 'Winning isn't everything. It's the only thing.'

Sir Alex Ferguson, Europe's most successful soccer coach, was once in the news due to a dressing room incident at Manchester United. The team had just lost a game and he was letting the players know how he felt about that. Apparently, in his temper he kicked a football boot across the dressing room and hit one of his star players, David Beckham, just above the eye.

Unfortunately the media present these situations and character traits as what makes a successful manager. Managers, and particularly those new to a leadership role, try to model themselves on those that they read about and see on TV.

In a recent seminar I asked a young manager why she thought Roy Keane played so well under Sir Alex Ferguson at Manchester United. 'It's because Alex regularly kicks his ass,' was her reply. Now Roy Keane is a real tough guy player known for his hard and uncompromising style on the soccer field. I asked this young manager how she thought Roy would respond to having his ass kicked regularly. She didn't seem to have an answer to that.

Managers are misreading the signs sent by the media and our culture and it's creating difficulty for them. Some managers can adopt the tough guy approach very easily but most feel uneasy with it. Those, who are uneasy, in an attempt not to be seen as weak, then manage their people in a way that makes them as a manager feel uncomfortable. This ultimately causes problems with their teams.

You can't make a silk purse from a sow's ear

My fourth point is that some people just don't have what it takes to be a manager. Just as some people don't have what it takes to be a doctor, a plumber, a lawyer or a bus driver. Whatever job or profession an individual ends up in doesn't mean to say it's the right one for them.

> *Some people just don't have what it takes to be a manager.*

Remember my story earlier about my first job as an apprentice engineer and how I was expected to make a hammer. I have a mechanical turn of mind so it was fairly easy for me to file a piece of steel and turn it into a hammer. Some of my fellow apprentices hadn't a clue and at that time I couldn't understand how they found it so difficult.

I caught my brother changing a wheel on his new Mini Cooper one day; he was having a great deal of difficulty. 'You're trying to screw the wheel nuts on in an anti-clockwise direction', I incredulously informed him. 'What's the difference?' he said. 'And what's anti-clockwise anyway?' My brother is a lovely guy and an extremely successful building surveyor, but please don't ask him to change a light bulb.

Of course, people can improve with training but we have to accept the fact that some will not. You can send a poor manager on a training course but they'll either reject everything they hear or they'll realise that they're in the wrong job.

When I was very much younger than I am now (about forty years younger) my father was determined that I would learn to play the piano. He went to the length of buying a piano in order that I could practise every day. My teacher, Miss Alexander, spent three long years trying to turn me into Liberace; to this day I cannot play a note. I realise now as an adult that I don't have an ear for music and I'm not particularly interested in listening to it, never mind playing an instrument. Attempting to train me to play a musical instrument is a near impossibility.

You may be starting to feel that perhaps being a manager is not for you and that may be the case. You'll obviously make your own decision about what track your career will take but I would ask you not to give up too easily. Although I've said that some managers are in the wrong job, they tend to be in the minority. If you feel that you're not having the success you should have, ask yourself if you've ever received any help. I think you'll find that like many managers, you've been left to get on with it. That's why I've written this book. So stick with the book before you make any decisions about your career as a manager.

So the job's difficult and you don't get any help, the media misleads you and some of us shouldn't even be in the job. Is there any good news? Of course there is. We're going to look at how to get better. But first, let's examine what the successful managers do, find out what we can learn from them and how we can get even better than them.

SUCCESSFUL MANAGERS DON'T MAKE IT HARD

Firstly we need to consider what we mean by a 'successful' manager. I believe that there are two factors that identify a successful manager:

1. A manager who gets the job done.

2. A manager who does it in the easiest and least stressful way possible.

Let's be totally clear about point 1: as a team manager you've got to achieve your target, your production figures or whatever it is that your organisation requires of you. It's one thing to have a happy motivated team; however, it's another thing if they're not 'doing the business'. If that's the case, then you're not a successful manager.

You also want to be able to go home at night in the knowledge that you've done what was required of you. That can be a great confidence booster and it also makes you feel good about yourself.

However, I'm sure that in being a successful manager and achieving your business goals, you don't want to kill yourself in the process. Too many managers are suffering from stress, losing sleep and damaging their family life. That's not what success is all about and I'm sure it's not what you want. Some managers seem to believe that stress and hassle is 'all part of the territory' and that they should just accept it.

I've known 'successful' managers in terms of achieving their business targets who were not successful in their personal life. How many marriages have suffered because one of the partners was spending too much time being successful in their job? How often has the relationship with our children suffered because of a lack of quality time spent with them?

> *How many marriages have suffered because one of the partners was spending too much time being successful in their job?*

I've know managers who've collapsed in the workplace due to stress. I'm sure you've also heard of sports coaches who've suffered heart attacks while watching a game.

It's been said that success has to come at a price. However, that price should not be paid in terms of a troubled personal life. We can pay the price of success by changing our viewpoint, increasing our knowledge of human nature and making changes to the way we lead our teams.

John Wooden, ex-UCLA basketball coach, was voted the best sports coach of all time in a recent poll. 'I had a successful basketball career,' he wrote in his 1997 book *Wooden*. 'But I believe I had an even more successful marriage.'

Successful managers get products out of the door or hit their sales target, and if they're in sport they win the championship. However, they also do it at the lowest possible personal cost to themselves and their families.

How do the good guys do it?

I've spent many years studying successful managers, whether they were in business or in sport, trying to establish what makes the good guys so good. I have absolutely no doubt in my mind that these managers and coaches know:

1. How to do all the business parts of the job.

2. How to do all the human parts of the job.

There's no doubt that a manager can have a certain level of success if they're good at the business part of the job but not so good at the human part. Some managers can go through their whole career by being competent in all the business and technical aspects of the job.

Does a sales manager need to know about selling? Of course she does. Does an IT manager need to know about computer hardware and software? Of course he does. Does a football coach need to know how to play football? Of course he does.

It's going to be pretty difficult to manage your team if you don't know how to do what your team members do. However, contrary to what some people believe, the successful manager doesn't have to be as good at the job or as knowledgeable as their team members.

If you look at the careers of some of our successful sports coaches you'll find some guys who were pretty average players. Many of them were nowhere near as good as some of the star players they coach today. However, that hasn't stopped them becoming successful as coaches.

It's important to have the knowledge about the industry or business that you're in and understand how your team members do their job. However, that's not what will ultimately determine your success as a manager.

Mike Krzyzewski, the basketball coach, says in his book *Leading with the Heart*: 'It's important for a leader to focus on the technical details of his industry or business. But it's *vital* to focus on details related specifically to people in the organization.'

To be a successful Motivational Manager you've got to know the business you're in, but more importantly you've got to know how to get the best out of your people.

To be a successful Motivational Manager you've got to know the business you're in, but more importantly you've got to know how to get the best out of your people. In my career I worked for seven companies, three of which I joined as an experienced manager. Of the three I joined as a manager, one sold car maintenance products, the next one sold tools and industrial supplies and the last one sold beer; three totally different industries with different customers and cultures.

I can remember some of my new team members saying to me at each company I joined, 'It's different in this business, you'll find it difficult because it's not the same as you're used to.' (Do you think they were pleased to see me?)

Of course it was a different industry but managing the team members wasn't different and that was what I was hired to do.

At interview stage, even senior managers had reservations about my lack of knowledge of their industry. However, when I joined these organisations I made it my business to find out as much as I could about the industry and the products. I never became an expert in the products or services but I sure knew how to manage their people, communicate with them on a human level and bring in the sales.

The ironic thing is that most organisations will help managers become better at the business factors but do very little if anything with the human aspects. And if you think about it any further it's probably the reason you bought this book.

Managers have traditionally developed the skills in finance, planning, marketing and production techniques. Too often the relationships with their people have been assigned a secondary role. This is too important a subject not to receive first line attention.

William Hewlett (1912–2001, American businessman, co-founder of Hewlett-Packard)

HOW TO WIN THE CHAMPIONSHIP

In my quest to find out what makes the good guys good I've read many reports and articles. I've read the books and watched the TV documentaries about successful sports coaches. Much has been said and written about these people and what made them successful. There's obviously a lot of comment about and emphasis on all the technical things they did and how they really knew the game they were in.

When you read what the players say about coaches when they write their autobiographies you'll obviously find comments about the technical aspects of the game. You'll discover how the coach was tough and competitive and how he drove the players hard. But you'll also hear many other comments which are not about the business side of the coach's activities but more about the human, and I believe this is where you'll find the real secret of their success.

Some of the comments I've read about coaches include:

John Wooden:

'One of the true gentlemen in sports or any other walk of life.'

'He taught them to be good people, good sports and still be competitive.'

Scotty Bowman:

'A great sense of humour that people never see.'

'Deep down, a caring man.'

Mike Krzyzewski:

'You cannot mistake the fact that he loves his players. He cares about their schooling and them being model citizens.'

'Coach K still puts up the wins proving once and for all nice guys can finish first.'

As I said earlier, I believe that the media misrepresents these coaches and what makes them successful. Of course they're tough and competitive; they make no bones about the fact that they must achieve their goals. However, they do that by demonstrating to their players that they care about each of them as individuals.

Sir Alex Ferguson recently celebrated his thousandth game in charge of Manchester United, probably the world's most successful soccer team. I don't think there's any doubt that Sir Alex does get angry when his team aren't performing, but there's another side to his personality that people don't see or don't want to see.

As Peter Schmeichel, the ex-Manchester United goalkeeper, said in a newspaper article, 'The kind and understanding side to his personality is something people outside United don't see. Fergie can be explosive, yet once he'd got a problem out into the open and dealt with it, it was gone. He never bore grudges. One minute he'd be furious, the next he'd ask – How's your family?'

Jose Mourinho, the Portuguese manager of Chelsea football club, is the world's highest-paid football manager. In an interview for *Men's Health* magazine, he was asked what quality was most important in contributing to his success as a manager. 'I think its love,' he replies. 'Love comes first, and because of love, other things arrive. I think without my love for my wife and for my kids, I wouldn't be the manager I am. I think life is about that.'

The *Men's Health* interviewer, John Naughton, goes on to say: 'Mourinho's love extends beyond his family: his love applies to his players as well, and in particular to John Terry and Frank Lampard. Mourinho speaks of them like favourite sons. He has undoubted love for them, as they, quite obviously, have for him.'

Here are some comments about coaches taken from an article in the US version of *Men's Health* magazine written by David Brooks and Chris Lawson:

Wayne Graham, baseball coach, Rice University: 'A demanding coach is redundant. If they are going to be happy with you and produce, they have to know you care.'

Frosty Westering, head football coach, Pacific Lutheran University: 'Both men and women have emotional needs. We all want to belong to a group. We all want to feel some worth, to know that people care about us and love us. When you can meet those needs for people, even in an aggressive, competitive arena, they'll respond with incredible effort.'

Are you tough enough?

The most important need for any human being is to feel cared about and accepted. We will do almost anything for someone who cares about us. We are drawn to and attracted by people who care about us.

Successful managers and sports coaches know that they need to care about their people if they are to get results and minimise their own stress levels. They are skilled at the human part of their job, they have emotional skills.

> *Successful managers and sports coaches know that they need to care about their people if they are to get results and minimise their own stress levels.*

Daniel Goleman is a psychologist and author of the international bestselling books *Emotional Intelligence* and *Working with Emotional Intelligence*. In his book *The New Leaders* he states: 'The fundamental task of leaders, we argue, is to prime good feelings in those they lead. At its root, the primal job of leadership is emotional.'

Goleman has his critics, particularly among those who think his is some sort of touchy-feely warm and fuzzy type of approach. Other critics see emotional intelligence or EQ as some sort of new buzz word or dippy theory.

You only have to look at the characteristics of emotional intelligence – self-awareness, self-regulation, motivation, empathy and social skill – and you'll find them in successful managers.

Many successful entrepreneurs also have high EQ. I'm thinking of people like Richard Branson, founder of the Virgin group of companies. People like Branson know how to make the emotional connection with their people.

Emotional intelligence isn't some new fad or psychologist's theory; it's just the factor that's been driving successful managers and coaches for years, except they weren't aware of it. However, they soon realised that to get the best out of their people they needed to concentrate on the human interactions and make that emotional connection. They discovered that you must be tough enough to be a Motivational Manager. Let's find out how to do it.

2
The Five Factors of Success

START THINKING IN A DIFFERENT WAY

I finished the last chapter by stating that many successful managers are good at human interactions with their people but sometimes aren't aware of how they do it. It's just a factor we have to accept – some people just have a natural talent for human interactions. You might have that talent, or then again you might have a natural talent for doing something else like accountancy, fixing a car engine or playing the violin.

Tiger Woods has a natural talent for playing golf, Al Pacino for acting and John Wooden for basketball coaching.

Now you might not be able to play golf like the Tiger, act like Pacino or coach the Wooden way, but I'm sure that with a bit of training you could improve in all of these areas.

I'm not much of a golfer so I went for some lessons some years ago. The Professional made me hold the club and stand in a way that made me feel really uncomfortable. For a while I hit nothing but huge chunks of turf, but after a bit of practice I started to hit the ball further and more accurately than I'd ever done before. All I needed was someone to show me what to do and coach me; however, I don't think I'll ever make Tiger nervous.

You might be feeling a bit uncomfortable with all this 'caring' and 'human' stuff, a bit like me holding the golf club. However, you're not alone; many managers feel the same way. When I first started as a manager I used to worry that my team would see me as too much 'Mr Nice Guy' and maybe a bit of a soft touch, and

I'm aware that's an issue that concerns a lot of managers. However, to be a Motivational Manager you're going to have to start thinking about this in a different way. I changed my way of thinking and I started to reap the benefits.

Remember the old saying: 'If you always do what you've always done, you'll always get what you've always got.'

On one of my recent seminars, we were talking about our human interactions and how our people need to know that we care. One manager said to me, 'My team know that I care about them.' So I asked him, 'What is it you do or say that lets them know that you care about them?' 'Oh I don't do or say anything, they just know,' was his reply.

Follow that line of thinking into your personal life and think about your relationship with your nearest and dearest. If you don't do or say anything to let the people in your life know that you care about them, don't be surprised if they suddenly disappear.

I like the saying: 'When should you tell your wife that you love her? Before somebody else does.' And ladies, that's not just a man thing.

> *You have to, say or demonstrate behaviour to your team members that lets them know you care about them.*

You have to, say or demonstrate behaviour to your team members that lets them know you care about them.

Now I know what you're thinking. Do have to tell them I love them? Should I buy them presents? Somehow I don't think so; however, you need to do something.

You need to start by breaking some old habits and establishing some new ones; you need to start thinking and acting in a different way.

Caring is a powerful business advantage.

Scott Johnson

Talk to yourself – they can't touch you for it

Thinking is all about communicating with yourself; it's all the little things you say to yourself while you're awake. I read somewhere that the average human has 12,367 thoughts every day. Now don't ask me how they worked that one out but let's just accept that we do a lot of thinking and communicating with ourselves.

The thing is that 70 per cent of these thoughts or internal conversations we have with ourselves are negative. If you don't believe me, consider for a moment what you say to yourself when you hear the following:

From your boss – 'I need to speak to you in my office.'

Do you think – 'Oh goody, I'm going to get a raise.'

From the person who shares your life – 'We need to talk.'

Do you think – 'I'm about to be told how wonderful I am.'

From the tax office – 'We need to have a meeting with you.'

Do you think – 'Great, I'm going to get a tax rebate.'

Of course you don't. You think that you're going to get fired, lose the love of your life and be hit by an unexpected tax bill.

Your thoughts will control your emotions and as a result, how you act. And just think how those statements above could affect your emotions and your stress level.

How you think – your relationship with yourself – is what's going to decide how well you communicate and relate to your team members and your boss. The most important relationship you'll ever have is with yourself, so you've got to get that right.

> *The most important relationship you'll ever have is with yourself, so you've got to get that right.*

Henry Ford (he was the guy who started all the traffic chaos) said, 'Thinking is the hardest work there is, that's why so few people do it.'

> *The Motivational Manager doesn't react, he thinks.*

Too often we don't think, and instead just react to how we feel. The Motivational Manager doesn't react, he thinks.

You have to get to know this person

For many years I've been fascinated by what makes people successful in their life, whatever it is they do for a living. I've read biographies, watched people being interviewed on television, studied newspaper and magazine profiles and spoken to many people who are successful in their fields of activity. I've been going on the premise that if I want to be successful then I need to do what successful people do. When these people are asked about success they usually define it as something that's personal to them; a feeling of contentment, achievement or happiness. However, what I'm interested in is, how do they get to that state? The conclusion I've come to is that there are five basic characteristics that successful people have. I like to call them –

THE FIVE FACTORS OF SUCCESS

1. Mind Control

Successful people have the ability to run their own mind. They don't let other people or circumstances run it for them. They re-programme their negative conditioning. They raise their level of self-esteem and they develop a positive attitude through continual positive self-talk. They don't react – they think!

2. Belief

Successful people have a passion for what they believe in. They set goals and achieve them by motivating themselves. They have vision.

3. Energy

They have lots of vroom! They manage stress and they know how to relax.

4. Rapport

They have the ability to communicate and get on with people, and to persuade people to accept their point of view.

5. Courage to act

People who make a success of what they do are willing to try. They're prepared to make mistakes, to assert themselves and not get too concerned about what others might think.

We're going to look at each of these Five Factors in turn.

FACTOR 1 – MIND CONTROL

Motivational Managers have a deep understanding of their own minds. They're aware of their needs, their strengths and weaknesses, and their emotions. They're honest with themselves and, with their team members.

You have to decide who runs your mind. Is it you or is it somebody else?

Let me give you an example. I've always had a thing about good timekeeping; it's something that's been programmed into my brain. If you agree to meet me at 8.30 in the morning, I'll be there at 8.20; I will always do my utmost be on time.

So I used to get angry when a member of my team would show up late for a meeting or an appointment with me. When I got angry I'd get stressed and end up saying something to the team member that I regretted later. Therefore, I learned to start thinking about the situation and tried to see it from their point of view and not let my programming run my brain.

That doesn't mean to say I ignored the lateness or did nothing about it; I thought very carefully about what I wanted to say and spoke to the team member about how we would resolve this situation. This is a very important area for us and we're going to look at it much closer in Chapter 5.

The point about this is I'm not prepared to allow that team member's behaviour to run my mind. Getting angry and stressed is not good for your health and it isn't a productive way to motivate your team.

I mentioned earlier about Sir Alex Ferguson kicking a football boot across the dressing room and hitting his star player in the face. Of course we want to see passion in a team leader but that sort of behaviour isn't healthy for Sir Alex and isn't motivational for the team. They know when they've played badly and getting hit by a flying football boot doesn't help the situation.

John Wooden, reckoned to be the best-ever sports coach in America, taught his players self-discipline and was his own best example. His demeanour was always contained. His philosophy was that if you needed emotion to make you perform then sooner or later you'd be an emotional wreck and then non-functional.

In running their own mind, Motivational Managers know what they're good at and what they're not so good at. Again it's important to be honest with yourself. Some managers take on tasks they're not good at, thinking that they should be able to do them. They then make a complete mess of it and 'beat themselves up' for being so useless.

> *Don't ever put yourself down; challenge and test yourself before deciding whether you can or cannot do something.*

On the other hand, don't ever put yourself down; challenge and test yourself before deciding whether you can or cannot do something.

I was once in a position to apply for an internal promotion. However, I didn't do it. I got it into my head that I wouldn't be able to handle the financial aspects of this new management position. When one of my colleagues, an accountant, asked me why I hadn't applied, I explained about the financial bit. She didn't pull her punches – 'You should have applied, you idiot. You would've been able to do the financial bit, it's not that difficult, and I would have helped you anyway.'

You can imagine how I felt after that. I had allowed some program in my brain to influence me and missed an opportunity for promotion. It's important to listen to that voice in your head which is driven by your programs, but also to challenge it.

When I now hear that voice in my head saying, 'You couldn't do that', I reply with, 'Well I'm going to give it a try before I decide.'

Motivational Managers have confidence in themselves. They accept their weaknesses but they don't see them as failures. They speak out when they don't know something and they ask for help when they need it.

> *Motivational Managers have confidence in themselves. They accept their weaknesses but they don't see them as failures.*

Have you ever asked a question at a meeting possibly feeling a bit stupid and thinking everyone else knows the answer? At the coffee break someone then says, 'I'm glad you asked that question because I didn't know either but I didn't like to ask.'

Motivational Managers have the courage to challenge what they hear in their own mind and also what they hear from other people.

Don't think too much

It's vital to run your own mind and think before you speak or take action. However, it's also important not to think too much. Sometimes you need to trust your instincts and your gut feelings.

If you're interviewing someone and your gut feeling is that this person isn't right for the job, then don't hire them. Too often, managers suppress their gut feeling. They think, 'I must be stupid, I'm probably wrong, they'll be okay once they've started working with me.' Trust me – they won't!

In his book *The Luck Factor*, Dr Richard Wiseman states, 'Lucky people make successful decisions by using their intuition and gut feelings.'

FACTOR 2 – BELIEF

The second of the Five Factors is Belief. It's dependent on how we control our mind and the conversations we have with ourselves. Belief in yourself is what drives your motivation and that in turn generates the energy to succeed. A manager who doesn't have belief in themselves or in what they are doing is going to find life very difficult. Of course, it can be challenging to retain a belief in yourself when you're under pressure from your manager and your team.

Fifteen years ago I was working for a brewery in the UK (yes, I did get lots of samples to take home). One day my manager, the Director of Sales, handed me a new challenge. The customer service telesales team were doing a mediocre job but had the potential to bring in for more sales. He told me to sort it out. I inherited a totally demotivated team of fourteen telesales agents and a supervisor whose job it was to phone customers in hotels, bars and restaurants and process their orders for beer, wine and other drinks.

John, the distribution manager I was taking over from, briefed me on my new team. 'They're a truculent bunch and they're always whingeing. There are always two or three of them off sick at any one time and you'll never get them to sell promotions.'

As you'll gather, it took a great deal of self-belief on my part to turn this team around. I was continually hearing from them and sometimes my manager, 'You can't do that Alan,' or 'That'll never work,' or 'We've never done it that way before.' I had many discussions with my manager and other senior managers regarding things I wanted to do to improve this team. I won some battles and I lost a few. However, I held on to my belief that I could make this team successful. It took me about six months to start turning things around – but I did it using the skills and techniques that I'll share with you in this book.

I said earlier that it's tough to hold onto belief in yourself when your manager and your team are telling you all the things you *can't* do. In Chapter 5 we'll look at how you communicate with your manager and your team, but first you must get that positive self-talk going and believe in yourself.

FACTOR 3 – ENERGY

The third of the Five Factors and something the Motivational Manager needs lots of. You need **brain energy** and you need **body energy**. However, as with any other kind of energy, it's constantly being drained away and needs replacing.

Managing people can drain both your brain and your body – and you probably don't need me to tell you that. How often have you gone home tired and stressed out and your partner says, 'I can't understand why you're so tired darling.' You then go on to try to explain about your hard day and try not to strangle them!

Remember what I said earlier: 'The Motivational Manager doesn't react; he thinks.'

> *Reacting drains the brain – thinking, less so.*

Reacting drains the brain – thinking, less so.

I gave an example earlier of your boss saying, 'I need to speak to you in my office.' If you react to that with, 'Oh no, what does she want, what have I done now? Maybe she wants to get rid of me', that sort of reaction drains your brain of energy and gives you stress.

So, get the thinking bit working and say to yourself, 'I'll speak to her now and see what she wants. If it's about the poor results, what information do I need to make my case? Perhaps she wants to talk about new plans for the team.'

Whatever you're thinking, **stop the negative stuff – it'll kill you!**

> *Whatever you're thinking, stop the negative stuff – it'll kill you!*

If one of your team comes to you with a problem or a customer complaint, start thinking, 'Let's see what I can do about this.' **Do not**, and I repeat, **do not** say 'Oh no, what am I going to do now?' Every time you say 'Oh no' your brain has a huge drain of energy and a whole cocktail of chemicals pumps into your system.

I just want to say a few more words about stress. People will tell you that there's good stress and bad stress. I'm talking about bad stress and it occurs when your brain is drained of energy. Some managers seem to believe that it 'goes with the territory' and some even wear it as a 'badge of honour'. They also believe that it can't be avoided; it's the fault of the company and the world we live in. Organisations do have a responsibility to minimise levels of stress in their workforce but you also have a responsibility for yourself.

It's very important to minimise your levels of stress and you can do that by thinking rather than reacting. Challenge your inbuilt programs. Stop saying, 'That makes me really mad' or 'That really gets on my nerves.' Start saying, 'This is something I have to deal with and I'll deal with it.' Remember – **you** have the choice.

I know you're probably thinking (or is it reacting), 'That's all very well Alan but it's hard sometimes not to get stressed.' You're absolutely right. However; let me give you some more reasons why you need to work at minimising it.

Stress can cause heart disease, sleeplessness, sexual problems, overeating, drinking too much, loss of concentration and stomach upsets. Research is now telling us that many, if not most, of our illnesses can be related to stress.

When we get stressed, one of the chemicals that are released into our bloodstream is called cortisol, sometimes known as the 'stress hormone'. High levels of cortisol can lead to diabetes and skin problems. There is also a suggestion that cortisol attacks our immune system and leaves us vulnerable to many of the bugs and viruses that come along.

So if you've ever suffered from skin complaints or perhaps too many colds, they could very well be the result of stress. I don't want to scare you to death or give you any more stress. I just want you to **think**.

I read a lot about stress some years ago and made a personal decision to decrease my levels of the bad stuff. When situations occur that are potentially stressful, I go into thinking mode to resolve them. I don't say, 'Oh no!' I say, 'Deal with it!'

I want to live a long and healthy life and I'm not prepared to let stress affect that; I recommend you do the same.

> *You don't get ulcers from what you eat. You get them from what's eating you.*
>
> Vicki Baum (1888–1960, American writer)

So what about the body stress? The body and the brain are linked together, so that when the brain drains of energy so does the body. However, the body does a lot of running about, up and down off the seat and often take a bit of a battering. For it to work well, it needs to be in good condition in the first place.

We should all know by now that if we eat too much or eat the wrong things, smoke too much or drink too much alcohol, then our body is in danger of breaking down.

Again it comes back to programming. I often tell people that I eat a lot of salad. The response – 'Salad is boring.' Not the way I make it, it isn't; I put all sorts of things into a salad other than the green ingredients – chillies, sun-blush tomatoes, anchovies, tuna, sardines, chicken, olives, cheese, sausage, etc. Not all at once, of course – I like a bit of variation on the theme. So open up your mind and open up the fridge, but be careful what you take out (of the fridge, that is).

If you want to be a Motivational Manager then you're going to have to do some exercise. Now I know you think you don't have the time. You may also be the type that doesn't want to go to the gym and lift heavy things or leap about in an aerobics class; however, you need to take some exercise that makes you sweat a little. I'm sorry, but a round of golf doesn't count – it isn't the kind of

> *If you want to be a Motivational Manager then you're going to have to do some exercise.*

exercise you need. Golf is great and it's good for the stress but it doesn't make you sweat. If you're going to walk then walk fast for a distance, enough to push up the heart rate and increase the breathing. (And don't run round the golf course with your clubs on your back – that's going too far.)

Again, get your internal program right and start to think how you can make your exercise enjoyable. I see some people at the health club making the whole business a real chore. They get on a bike or a rowing machine and try to kill themselves for twenty minutes. If that's your thing then fine, but please don't make it a chore – plug into the sound system and catch up with what's on TV. I like to do circuit classes with a whole group of people, many of whom have become friends. I enjoy the chat before-hand, the music and the exercise (and I also like the fact that there are more girls than guys).

If you're really not into exercise then please make sure that you have other activities outside of your workplace and make them fun. Too many managers are going home and slumping in front of the TV; Motivational Managers don't do that.

So look after the body and the brain and you'll have lots of vroom!

FACTOR 4 – RAPPORT

Motivational Managers are good at building rapport and communicating with their team, as well as all the other people they come into contact with. Of course, communicating isn't just about speaking to your team. It's about listening and understanding how the team member sees the situation; it's also about being able to empathise and understand how they feel.

There were two ways I could have looked at my telesales team:

1. As John, the outgoing manager, had described them – a bunch of troublesome underachievers.

2. As reasonable human beings who wanted to do a good job.

I chose the latter.

Again it comes back to the same question: Who runs your mind? Is it you or is it somebody else? It would have been so easy to accept John's description of this team; after all, he was a nice guy and he'd worked with them for a while. The only thing is, he wasn't a very good manager. I could understand how the telesales agents felt in their jobs. If I'd been managed the way they'd been, I'd probably have taken days off work and complained a lot more.

See it how they see it

When you have to deal with a team member who's complaining to you, rather than allowing your negative programs to take over, get your thinking part in gear and try to see the situation the way your team member sees it. You don't necessarily have to agree with them but perhaps you can empathise with their point of view.

The Motivational Manager thinks about the people in her team, she's sensitive to how they see things and knows that they might think differently from her.

> *The Motivational Manager thinks about the people in her team, she's sensitive to how they see things and knows that they might think differently from her.*

I mentioned earlier about timekeeping and I know many people don't see it as importantly as I do. We all see the world in a different way based on our culture and how we were brought up. So it's very important to understand this, particularly when you give your people feedback, be it good or bad.

A few years back I spent several weeks in a particular hotel running seminars and I started to get to know some of the staff. One day I noticed that Carol the conference manager had been named employee of the month and her photograph was displayed in the reception area. When I congratulated her on this honour I was a bit surprised at her reaction. 'I hate it, I'm so embarrassed,' she complained. Carol didn't like the attention she was getting, and as a result this recognition by her manager didn't motivate her. Another member of the team could possibly see this completely differently and regard it as a great honour. It would have been far better if Carol's manager had spoken with her in private and thanked her for all her good work.

> *The Motivational Manager understands each team member and doesn't reward everyone in the same way.*

If you have good rapport with your team members then you become sensitive to how they see things. The Motivational Manager understands each team member and doesn't reward everyone in the same way.

I've often heard managers say, 'I treat people the way I expect to be treated.' The Motivational Manager says, 'I treat people the way **they** expect to be treated.'

I was smiling to myself as I read the sign on the wall in the men's room at the offices of one of my clients recently. It said, 'PLEASE LEAVE THESE FACILITIES THE WAY YOU WOULD EXPECT TO FIND THEM.' I was smiling because I've been in bathrooms in people's houses over the years. Soap everywhere, towels lying on the floor and not as clean as I would like. So how would these people react to the notice on the men's room wall?

It *is* what you say and *how* you say it

As well as listening and understanding, it's obviously important to speak to your people. I say obviously. However, I've known managers who say very little to their people other than to issue instructions, and they're often not clear with these.

Some years ago a large and successful football club appointed a new coach. He replaced a coach who had gone on to bigger and better things. This successful team started to go downhill from day one; they were losing games to much lesser teams on a regular basis.

The new coach had been successful as a player and had worked as an assistant coach at another team. Did he know the business he was in? Did he know about football? Of course he did. Did he know how to speak to the media and more importantly his team? I'll leave you to answer that one.

The newspaper, radio and TV people didn't like this new coach because of his offhand manner towards them; the players felt the same and it showed in their results.

If you want to motivate your team and achieve the team's goals, then you've got to talk to them on a human as well as a business level.

> *It's not enough just to issue instructions; you've got to get to know your individual team members.*

It's not enough just to issue instructions; you've got to get to know your individual team members.

Get off your 'butt'

I've often heard managers say, 'My door is always open, come and talk to me anytime.'

You have to accept the fact that your team won't always do that. They might not want to bother you or they may feel that they should know the answers to their questions and they'll look stupid if they ask. And how many times have they approached you and you've been on the phone or 'too busy'? It's your job to get out and talk to them.

I've also heard managers say, 'I sit with my team in an open-plan office so I'm always available to them and I hear what's going on.' **Oh no you don't!**

It's important to get out of your office or up off your seat and mix with the team on a regular basis.

> *It's important to get out of your office or up off your seat and mix with the team on a regular basis.*

Don't wait for them to come to you. Pull up a chair and have a chat and don't just talk about business – find out how they're doing on a human level. That doesn't mean prying into their personal life, but your team members want to feel that you're interested and care about them as individuals.

It's also important that they feel free to chat among themselves, so don't stifle that. A team who have good relationships with each other are a productive team.

Many managers aren't comfortable about speaking to their team members unless it's about business. I've worked for many managers who knew nothing or very little about me on a personal basis.

One of my colleagues once told me that our manager had asked him if I was gay. He'd come to this conclusion because there didn't seem to be a woman in my life. At the time he was coming to this conclusion, I was going through the break-up of my fifteen-year marriage to my wife. However, my manager didn't know that nor would he have been able to handle it if he did. That doesn't suggest he was a bad person, he just didn't know how to make that human connection and sadly he didn't try.

Perhaps you're not comfortable speaking to your team on a human level, so that's why we're going to take a closer look at what to say in Chapter 5. However, for the moment I would ask that you consider the importance of your communication and rapport-building skills. Your success as a manager is highly dependent on your ability to listen to and speak with your people. Human beings crave attention and acceptance and they want to know you care. If your team members feel that you're interested and care about them as individuals, then it becomes so much easier for you to achieve your goals.

Successful entrepreneurs are excellent at building rapport. When you meet them they don't necessarily talk about themselves, they ask *you* questions. I've met several successful business people and I'm always impressed and flattered by their interest in me.

You can practise your rapport-building skills any time, particularly in your personal life. In the locker room at my local health club, I notice that many of the guys don't speak to each other. I always make a point of saying hello or passing the time of day. If they don't want to talk then that's fine. However, I find they usually do and I've had some interesting conversations.

Speak to everyone you meet and practise your rapport-building skills: taxi drivers, people in trains, on aeroplanes and anywhere else you come into contact. I sometimes have to push myself to do it but I'm always glad when I do.

FACTOR 5 – COURAGE

Factor 5 in my list of success characteristics is the courage to act. You're going to need a lot of courage to be a really successful manager. You need courage to run your own mind, and to question and possibly change your programming.

Christine, the supervisor of the telesales team I described earlier, phoned me one day: 'I want to have a bit of a celebration on Friday afternoons', she said. 'I want to celebrate the team's success for the week and have some chocolates, cake and wine.'

Now I have a program (call me old-fashioned) that tells me, 'No alcohol in the workplace,' it's a big no-no. However, I thought about it for a second, cancelled the 'no alcohol' program in my brain and told Christine to go ahead. However, there was still a bit of me (these programs can be very powerful) that thought I was maybe doing the wrong thing. Perhaps they would get drunk and insult the customers or other colleagues, and what would my manager say?

Needless to say, the Friday afternoon session was a big success and the ironic thing is that everyone on the team was so busy working that they hardly had any time to eat the cake or drink the wine. I was glad I'd had the courage to challenge my programming.

As well as challenging *your* own programming, you're going to need courage to deal with difficult situations in your team. You need the courage sometimes to say 'no' and still keep the team motivated. In your communications with your manager you'll often need the courage to stand up for what you believe to be right.

> *As well as challenging* your *own programming, you're going to need courage to deal with difficult situations in your team.*

I once had a manager say to *me*, 'Alan, I'm going to promote this guy from another department into your sales team.' Coolly and calmly, I informed my manager that I'd interviewed this individual and I didn't think he was suitable for my sales team. I reminded my manager that in order to produce the results he required I needed to be sure that I had the best people for the job in my team. After a bit of wrangling I won this particular 'discussion', but as I said earlier, you don't win them all. However, you must have the courage to try.

I read somewhere 'Winners make mistakes but losers never do.' That's because winners have the courage to try and they know they'll make mistakes. However, that's how they learn and move forward.

So these are the Five Factors of Success; I'll refer back to them as we go through the book. Your success as a Motivational Manager is highly dependent on your ability to implement these factors.

Here are some other points I'd like you to consider before we move on.

YOU CAN'T MAKE PEOPLE WHAT THEY'RE NOT

Too many managers are spending too much time trying to change people. They seem to believe that if they train people, tell them what to do or threaten them with the sack, then they can get them to change.

The Motivational Manager concentrates on developing the strengths of his team members – not trying to correct their weaknesses. Sometimes you have to manage around a weakness (we'll look at that later) but you can't make people what they're not.

> *The Motivational Manager concentrates on developing the strengths of his team members – not trying to correct their weaknesses.*

I described earlier how I had taken some golf lessons. A friend and I spent some hours with a professional golfer and coach at a local country club. This was really useful to me and I did get better. However, my friend Robin hadn't a clue. No matter what the pro told him to do, how to change his stance and his grip, he could hardly hit the ball. If you'd given Robin a hundred lessons and threatened him with a gun, I doubt if he'd ever have completed a round of golf in less than two days. Robin is a successful lawyer and makes a lot of money. However, a golfer he is not!

So if you have a sales person on your team who isn't bringing in the sales or a production engineer who isn't making his quota then you have to make a decision (back to the thinking part). Is this person not producing because they don't have the ability, because they need more training, or because there's another reason?

We're going to look at coaching and other reasons for non-performance in Chapter 5 but for the moment it's important to understand that the individual may not be able to do the job. They may tell you they can do the job because they're unwilling to accept defeat. However, I've known people in sales jobs who shouldn't be in sales and doctors, plumbers, lawyers and engineers who were also in the wrong job.

What you need to do is get people who *can't* do the job into a job that they *can* do or get them out of your team.

I joined three companies as a manager and in each case I inherited team members who didn't have what it takes to do the job. I'd usually find three categories of people in the teams. The first group were the 'good guys', the ones I knew could do the job and wouldn't give me any hassle. The second group consisted of people who needed a bit of looking after, watching closely and definitely some coaching. The third group were the ones who didn't have either the skills or the characteristics to do the job and no amount of training, or anything I could do, would change that. I would often find that these people, due to their lack of success, weren't exactly happy in the job anyway and were sometimes only too pleased to be transferred to another position.

I hear you saying, 'Easier said than done Alan' and you're right. But the Motivational Manager needs to address these issues for the good of the team and the business. It often takes co-operation from your manager so we'll look at that in Chapter 5.

Strengths not weaknesses

I keep talking about Chapter 5 and that's where we'll look at how to give feedback. We'll be looking at how to give your team members (and your manager) feedback on their strengths and also on their weaknesses. However, these will only be weaknesses that we know the individual can do something about. It's a waste of your time and effort trying to sort weaknesses that can't be sorted. Some people just can't build relationships with customers, others can't work as fast as you need them to and others can't write a report to save their life.

> *Your most productive time as a manager will be spent giving feedback on strengths and how to develop these even further.*

Your most productive time as a manager will be spent giving feedback on strengths and how to develop these even further.

Many managers spend the majority of their time with team members trying to resolve weaknesses. They then don't have the time or sometimes the capability to give feedback on strengths. The Motivational Manager concentrates on strengths not weaknesses.

> *The Motivational Manager concentrates on strengths not weaknesses.*

One company where I worked as a regional sales manager had very strict procedures on how a field sales person should conduct themselves. They had to present the sale to a customer in a particular structured way. They had to dress in a certain way and do their paperwork in a certain way. Their car had to be clean and their product samples had to be laid out in the boot of their car in the 'company' way.

My boss, the General Sales Manager, was a stickler for these rules and regulations. However, needless to say, certain sales people in my team didn't always do their paperwork on time or have their car laid out in the required way. They *did*, however, bring in the sales and as their manager that was the outcome I needed from them. Therefore, I was extremely careful how I gave them feedback on their performance. I knew that I'd ultimately be judged by my manager on the sales performance of my team, so I concentrated on reinforcing their skills in that area. I didn't ignore untidy paperwork or samples that weren't laid out properly but I definitely kept any comments to the absolute minimum. I've witnessed a salesman, in another team, handing a big order to his manager and then being reprimanded for having an untidy car boot. If that's the approach you take, then what you end up with is tidy car boots and fewer sales.

Focus on the outcomes

As a manager you need to be very clear about what your outcomes are. Whether you call them goals, objectives or targets, these are the factors that you're ultimately judged on. You'll find them in your job description or contract and I'm sure your manager will concentrate on them at your next performance review. It's what you're paid to do.

Many managers allow themselves to be distracted and diverted from their outcomes. They get involved in all sorts of situations that take their 'eye off the ball'.

I regularly run a workshop for managers called *Managing Your Priorities*. At the start of the workshop I ask the managers to draw a map on a large sheet of flip-chart paper of all the things they do in their job. They almost inevitably fill that page with all sorts of tasks and activities. More often than not they surprise themselves with what's on the page. I then ask them to identify and mark with a large cross their real priorities, and the outcomes that they're ultimately judged on. Out of all the tasks and activities on the page they usually cross only five or six priorities and sometimes fewer. (You might want to try this exercise yourself sometime.)

What we do find, however, is that the priorities they identify are not allocated the time they deserve on a day-to-day basis. The managers will often blame their senior manager for many of the tasks that divert them from their priorities, which is perfectly fair. However, there are many tasks managers take on because:

1. They don't like to say 'no'.

2. They don't trust anyone else to do them.

3. They just 'like' to do the tasks themselves.

I then spend time in the workshop showing managers how to communicate with their senior manager and their other colleagues in order to minimise the number of tasks that don't contribute to their outcomes. It's back again to who runs your mind; is it you or is it somebody else?

Many managers fall into the trap of believing that their manager will understand why they haven't hit their target or quota. They seem to think that because the senior manager has handed out all sorts of other tasks, then they'll accept your failure to achieve your target. Well let me tell you now – they won't!

> *Motivational Managers keep focused on outcomes and don't allow anyone or anything to divert them without good reason.*

Motivational Managers keep focused on outcomes and don't allow anyone or anything to divert them without good reason.

Keep the team focused on outcomes

It's also important to focus on outcomes as far as your team is concerned. Whatever tasks your manager is putting on you, don't allow yourself to do the same to your team. Sometimes your team members will be only too happy to do other little jobs and tasks that you ask them to do. I've had sales people say, 'Oh, I'll deliver that to the customer, it's on my way.' Customer service people will say, 'I'll go and talk to distribution or finance department about that.' You have to keep asking yourself the question 'Is what they're doing helping me to achieve my outcomes?' If the answer is 'no', don't let them do it.

Make it clear to your team what the outcomes are and don't concern yourself too much about how they get there. Now that doesn't mean that you encourage a salesman to get a sale at any cost, or a chef to use inferior ingredients. And you obviously don't want a maintenance engineer cutting corners that could jeopardise safety. However, it does mean using your thinking part again and listening to your inbuilt programs. Your people may not do a job the way you would do it but that doesn't necessarily mean it's wrong.

I've often listened to a sales person speaking to a customer and found myself thinking, 'That's not the way I'd do it.' The temptation is to jump into the conversation or speak to the sales person afterwards. However, I've learned to keep my mouth shut, because many times the sales person closed the business, the customer was happy and it probably *was* better than I would do it.

I checked into a hotel recently and as I signed the paperwork the bubbly receptionist complimented me on my cologne. She asked what kind it was so that she might buy some for her boyfriend. Now I know this hotel chain and this isn't part of the welcoming speech. I also know that some managers would discourage this level of familiarity between staff and customers. But I'll tell you something as a customer – I loved it, and she certainly brightened my day! Her response was far better than some of the stuffy robotic greetings you get from receptionists at the major hotel chains.

This receptionist had made me a happy customer and if I owned this hotel that's an outcome I would want.

Southwest Airlines in the USA has consistently won awards for the fewest complaints, best baggage handling and best on-time performance. However, everything at Southwest is focused on fun. Obviously safety is important and all employees follow FAA regulations. But the whole purpose of the company is to have fun.

I've flown with airlines who continually tell me that their focus is my safety. I don't really want to know that; I take it as a given. **Stop telling me how safe I am, you're scaring me – I want fun!**

Southwest issue guidelines to flight attendants in their training courses. They hand out joke books and give them ideas and tools for having fun. They then leave it up to the individual flight attendant to create 'fun' for the customer. As they say, 'We don't want clones.'

The successful manager defines the outcomes to the team members and then lets each person find their way of getting there. That doesn't mean you walk away nor have no idea what's going on. As I said earlier, you should be constantly getting out there with the team, watching and listening and supporting what they're doing.

> *The successful manager defines the outcomes to the team members and then lets each person find their way of getting there.*

In Chapter 1 I said that the two characteristics of Motivational Managers were:

1. They get the job done.

2. They do it in the easiest and least stressful way.

I'm just reminding you of that, because to try to control your team's activities and get them to do things the way you want them done is extremely stressful. It can also mean that you demotivate the team and then it will be much harder to achieve your outcomes.

Trust your team

I just want to say a bit more about trusting and having faith in your people; it's so important that I've devoted Chapter 6 to it. However, this chapter is devoted to you and your characteristics and it's very important to get the 'trust' program into your brain. The old-style managers that I described in Chapter 1, were programmed to believe that they couldn't trust their people. That doesn't mean they thought they were dishonest, just that they needed to constantly supervise their people to ensure they did the job properly. Sadly, many managers still see it that way today.

The Motivational Manager thinks the opposite: he or she believes and trusts their people to do the job and let's them get on with it. If you've got the old program, as I once did, then be prepared to change it. Because if your team members believe that you trust them to do the job, then it will have a huge positive effect on morale and on you achieving your outcomes.

This book is all about how to become a Motivational Manager. However, as you've probably realised, *you* don't motivate your team – *you* create the environment in which they motivate themselves. Trusting your people to do their job goes a long way towards creating that environment.

> You *don't motivate your team – you create the environment in which they motivate themselves.*

However, you've firstly got to get the right people in your team and that's what we're going to look at next.

> *Trust is the lubrication that makes it possible for organizations to work.*
>
> Warren G. Bennis (1925–, American psychologist, management educator and consultant)

3
Pick the right people

KNOW WHAT YOU'RE LOOKING FOR

The time will come when you will need to interview someone to join your team. This could be someone currently working within your company or it could be an external candidate. Whatever the situation, you're going to have to make a decision about whether they're suitable for the job or not.

I'm aware that in some organisations a middle manager may have a new team member picked for them. The applicant is either hired by the Human Resources Department or the senior manager. If you're in this situation you must fight against it by communicating with your manager. You may want to leap ahead to Chapter 5 where we look at how to give feedback to your manager about situations such as this.

> *It will be extremely difficult to be a Motivational Manager unless you decide who'll be on your team.*

It will be extremely difficult to be a Motivational Manager unless *you* decide who'll be on your team. You need to have total faith and belief in every member of your team and they need to know that.

It may be the case that you work for an organisation that uses sophisticated selection systems such as psychometric testing. Or you might work for a small company where you write the job advertisement, do all the interviewing and make the coffee. Whatever the situation, there will come a time when you will be eyeball to eyeball with a potential team member.

Before you can ask a question or conduct an interview, you need to be very clear in your own mind about exactly what you're looking for. Now you might jump in here and say, 'I know what I'm looking for – a new receptionist or a maintenance engineer or a sales agent, and I want a good one.' But what do you mean by a 'good one'?

In the previous chapter we looked at the importance of achieving your outcomes. In order to do this you need people in your team:

1. Who can deliver the outcomes you need;

2. Who will fit with the company structure;

3. Who will fit with the existing team;

4. Who will respond to your style of managing;

5. Who will be happy in the job.

Let's look at each of these points in turn.

1. Outcomes

These could be more orders, or more happy customers, or fast maintenance turnaround; it's what you and your team are judged on. You need to be clear in your own mind as to the outcomes you need.

A telecom company that I work with employs engineers to repair and maintain telephone systems. This company has always employed people who are technically competent and can do all the screwdriver and wire-stripper stuff. However, it isn't enough to be technically competent nowadays; this organisation needs engineers who can interact with customers in a positive way. These engineers visit homes and offices and the interactions they have with customers will have an effect on their levels of customer service. In fact, positive customer interactions are now as important as fixing the phone.

If you were a manager interviewing engineers for this company, you would have to consider the applicants' interpersonal skills.

A few years back I was approached by a beer-brewing company regarding customer service training. They had suddenly come to realise that the employees who spent the most time face to face with the customers were the delivery drivers. Up until then, all customer service training had been directed at sales people and office staff, who often had irregular contact with the customers. The drivers were speaking with the customers once and sometimes twice a week. So it made a lot of sense to employ people who, as well as delivering the beer efficiently, could also be trained to make the customers feel special.

I spend a great deal of my time in hotels usually operated by one of the big chains. The first and last person you speak to in these hotels is the receptionist. I'm often surprised at the poor response from some of these receptionists. I've been welcomed by highly efficient people behind the desk who process me quickly and effectively; however, they're often about as warm as an Eskimo's ice cream. They don't make me feel welcome and they don't make me want to return. I would have thought these were two very important outcomes required from a hotel receptionist. However, I suspect they were employed primarily on their academic qualifications and their ability to 'process' customers.

2. Company structure

You also need to consider if the person you interview will be happy in your company and your culture. Some people who move from a large company to a much smaller one often find it hard to adjust.

Some years ago I moved from a large international organisation to a small local company. I went into the job with my eyes open and had three successful years. However, I often felt frustrated in the smaller company mainly by its culture and the way it went about its business; I was glad when I moved back to a bigger organisation. I just wasn't a 'small company' person.

I've interviewed people in a similar situation. I remember one lady who I interviewed for a sales agent's job at one of my clients. She was keen to get the job, she had loads of experience, all the skills required and I was confident that she could do it.

However, when describing her current job with a large company it became very apparent that she wouldn't fit into this smaller one. She kept talking about all the things they did in her present company and how she went about her daily duties. I knew that this job she was applying for was totally different from what she'd been used to. If I had employed her I believe that she wouldn't have been happy, would have ended up not doing a good job and would have probably spent her time trying to find a new position.

3. The team

Will the job applicant fit well with the existing team? Maybe your team are a group of loners who don't communicate with each other, but it's unlikely. You can't pick people who are all the same; you don't want a set of clones in your team. However, you need to pick someone who is on the same wavelength as the rest of the team. Perhaps you could involve a team member at a second interview; they might have a better feel for whether the person would fit in or not.

4. Your style of managing

How will the person respond to you? Will they be able to work with your style of management?

I've had applicants complain about their existing boss, 'Do you know that he expects me to do such and such.' And I've thought to myself, 'That's exactly what I'd be expecting as well.'

You've got to have a good connection with the person that you bring into your team. That doesn't mean to say that you're going to be best buddies, but you'll need to be able to work together.

Consider if you're the kind of manager who likes to work closely with your team and regularly check their progress. If so, you'll need an individual who wants structure and detail and is comfortable with close monitoring.

If, on the other hand, you're the kind of manager who sets outcomes and leaves the team to get on with it without much help from you, you're going to need someone who's happy to work with minimum supervision.

I once made a mistake with a guy I appointed into a field sales job. Because he was a college graduate I felt that he would be able to pick up the knowledge and selling skills really fast. I'm the second type of manager I described above. I tell people what the outcomes are and let them find their way to achieving them. I keep in contact and give feedback when they do well and also when they need to improve things.

However, this guy was at me all the time: 'What do I do next, where do I go now, how do I do it?' This of course took up too much of my time. The others in the team made decisions themselves and regularly checked with me. This guy was a 'bad fit', it didn't work and he left very soon of his own accord.

5. They need to be happy

Job applicants don't know what they're getting into when they start a new job. They might *think* they know but how can they when they've never worked in your team or your company before? Just as it's a risk for you when you start someone new, it's also a risk for them. You'll never totally eliminate the risk but it's your job to minimise the risk for both you and the applicant.

I think I'd like Jay Leno's chat show job on NBC. It must be great to sit and chat to glamorous movie stars and other interesting people. You don't even have to do much talking, you just ask a few questions and let them get on with it. You read a few jokes off the auto-prompter – no problem – and you get paid lots of money. But maybe it wouldn't suit me; perhaps I'd get bored in a few weeks. Maybe there are lots of tedious jobs they'd ask me to do behind the scenes. And I'd probably get bored with all the beautiful women who'd be throwing themselves at a famous person like me. On reflection, I'm willing to risk it; when's he leaving?

I've seen too many people start a new job and then find that it doesn't suit them, they don't like it and they want out. It causes problems for you as the manager; so I suggest you do every thing you can to avoid it.

WHAT YOU'RE REALLY, REALLY LOOKING FOR

Let's consider the factors you'll need to look for to find the right person for your team.

Imagine that you're a sports coach and you need a new player on the team. Would you walk up to someone in the street and say, 'I want you to come and play for my team. I'll train you to become the best player in the country'? Sounds a bit ridiculous, doesn't it? You'd obviously go and watch players in other teams. On the other hand, you might decide to find some young player that you could develop for your team. So you'd spend some time watching the kids in school.

What are you looking for when you're watching these kids or more established players? Is it experience of the game, or perhaps an all-round knowledge of how it should be played, or even just a good all-round player? All of these would be good to have but what you're really looking for is – **talent!**

> *What you're really looking for is – talent!*

You're looking for that gift or flair or capacity to achieve your outcomes. If you're looking for a goalkeeper, then you're looking for someone with that extra something that keeps the opposition from scoring. If you're looking for a shooter or a winger or a quarterback then it's the same story – you're looking for talent. It doesn't really matter how long they've been a player or whether they have a great knowledge of the game, you just need them to produce results.

It's no different when you're picking someone new for your team – you're looking for talent.

- The talent to strip down an engine and rebuild it in record time.
- The talent to make other people feel at ease.
- The talent to produce reports that are clear and easy to read.

It comes back to outcomes again; I can't emphasise this enough. Be absolutely clear what you need this person to do – keep in the forefront of your mind the outcomes you'll ultimately be judged on.

There is no substitute for talent. Industry and all the virtues are of no avail.

Aldous Huxley (1894–1963, British author)

I was having a cup of coffee with Mike, a friend of mine, in a local coffee shop. We were discussing the young lady who was serving us. 'I don't like her approach,' says Mike. 'She's not very friendly.' Now if I was to give this young lady the benefit of the doubt, I'd probably say she was a bit shy and had difficulty communicating with people. She just wanted to take our order and serve it when it was ready.

I asked Mike, 'What would you do if it was your coffee shop? What sort of person would you employ as a server?' 'Oh, I'd look for a girl with a bit of experience as a server, someone who looks clean and tidy and who's a nice pleasant person.'

I told Mike what I'd look for: 'Someone who would make the customers want to buy some more coffee or food, who'd make the customer want to come back and who'd probably recommend my coffee shop to other people.'

Now you may think that Mike and I are saying the same thing – the characteristics that he's looking for will bring the results I'm looking for. Yes, that may happen but I suspect that the server in this coffee shop displayed all of these characteristics when she was interviewed for the job. However, she wasn't going to cause Mike or I to return to this coffee shop or recommend it to others.

I also suspect that the owner of this coffee shop doesn't take as much care as they should when employing a server. There's probably the attitude from the owner that this isn't a very prestigious job or one that pays very well, so you can't be too fussy in who you employ.

I'm fed up with the saying, 'If you pay peanuts you'll get monkeys.' Low wages does not always equate to poor or mediocre performance. Remember what I said in Chapter 2 about changing our thinking. This is what I'm talking about.

I've been served by people in bars, restaurants and coffee shops who had all the characteristics that I described earlier – they made me want to spend more money, they made me want to come back and they certainly caused me to recommend to others. These people are out there; your job is to find them.

Intelligence won't do it

One of the programs that was installed in my brain as I grew up was that 'intelligent' people could do almost anything due to the fact that they had the capacity to learn. The education system when I was young was based on the understanding that if you left school with a whole raft of qualifications, any job was open to you. If you wanted to be a doctor, lawyer, pilot, engineer or architect, all you needed was these school qualifications and you could go on to learn anything.

Sadly, many people who did train to be doctors didn't turn out to be very good doctors, as with lawyers, pilots or any other job you care to mention. When I was an apprentice engineer I can remember working with young engineering college graduates. Some of them were very good, they had a talent for engineering and it was really apparent. However, there were others who, if truth be told, were pretty hopeless. Their intelligence had helped them learn enough information to qualify for a degree in engineering but they just didn't have the talent.

I mentioned earlier about the college graduate that I appointed as a sales person. I fell into the trap of not thinking but reacting to my programming and believing that because he was 'intelligent' he could learn to sell. He had the capacity to learn all about our products but he didn't have the talent to persuade others, or to go out and find customers.

I was also stupid enough to believe I could teach him. However, as I said in Chapter 2, you can't make people what their not.

You can teach people skills and give them knowledge. However, if they don't have the talent, their performance will suffer.

> *You can teach people skills and give them knowledge. However, if they don't have the talent, their performance will suffer.*

The motivational manager looks for intelligence, but more importantly he looks for talent to achieve the outcomes.

Experience won't do it either

A job applicant's previous work experience is often used to judge whether or not they have the capacity to do the new job. Many managers go through the CV discussing each previous job with the applicant. The applicant then goes on to tell the manager how clever they are and how successful they were in all their previous jobs.

It's almost a case of: 'Have you worked in our industry before?' – 'Yes, I have lots of experience in your industry' – 'Great, can you start on Monday?'.

I've been in the situation of interviewing someone for a sales job and they have several similar jobs on their CV. I've often asked myself, 'Who on earth employed this person in a sales job? I have no confidence in their ability whatsoever.'

Put your customer hat on for a moment and think about the people you've dealt with in the past who were pretty hopeless. The sales people, the plumbers, the maintenance engineers, or the customer service people on the end of the phone. When these people were interviewed for their job, they probably discussed with the interviewer their experience, how good they were in their current job and all their previous jobs. However, based on your interactions with them, I bet you'd have something to add to that discussion.

<table>
<tr><td>*Experience shouldn't be ignored, but it's not a reliable indicator as to whether someone can give you the outcomes you want.*</td></tr>
</table>

Experience shouldn't be ignored, but it's not a reliable indicator as to whether someone can give you the outcomes you want.

> *I'd rather have a lot of talent and a little experience than a lot of experience and a little talent.*

John Wooden (1910–, American basketball coach)

SEND FOR THE FAMOUS FIVE

So you're looking for talent, but what does that really mean? What are the factors we need to look for and how do we wangle them out? We'll come to a bit of wangling later but for the moment let's consider the talents we're looking for. Obviously every job will require different talents but there are some guidelines you can follow, so it's back to the Famous Factors of Success (you've heard about them before so they must be famous).

We've looked at the value of the Five Factors (Mind Control – Belief – Energy – Rapport – Courage, in case you've forgotten) and we've considered their importance in ensuring your success. If you think about it, the Five Factors are all talents. They aren't about skill or knowledge; they're about something within you that can be cultivated and grown. So you can use your knowledge of the Five Factors as a guide to identifying talents in your job applicants.

Mind control

Old-style management doesn't encourage mind control: employees aren't encouraged to think. That was certainly the case when I started work back in the bad old days. However, it's still prevalent in many businesses today.

It's evident in many of the organisations that I work with that there's a culture of 'I'm the boss – I tell you what to do – you don't question it.'

The Motivational Manager doesn't react that way, she employs people who **think**; people with a mind of their own who aren't afraid to say what they think and feel. You need people who question, who challenge you as a manager. Now I know you're getting scared, but remember the fifth of the Five Factors – Courage!

> *You need people who question, who challenge you as a manager.*

I remember sitting in on a second interview with a manager colleague of mine who was interviewing candidates for a sales job. One of the candidates was a guy called Phil; he was a very strong character, full of questions and suggestions on how the job should be done. John, the manager, turned to me when Phil left the room: 'That guy's good, I reckon he'd be a good salesman for us, but I don't think I could handle him.' John, was a much quieter type of person than Phil and I knew he felt uncomfortable with his style. So I asked John, 'What do you want this new salesman to do?' 'I want him to bring in new business.' 'Do you think he can do that?' I asked. 'Of course I do, I just think he'll be difficult to handle.'

Again, it all comes down to outcomes; of course, you've got to consider how you're going to work with a new team member but you sometimes need that courage to take a risk. John hired Phil and he brought in the new business that John needed. Phil always was a handful and a challenge for John but they learned to work together.

Just in case you think I'm always talking about sales, I was recently reading an article in a management magazine about some shop floor workers in a specialist engineering factory. Off their own bat and without being asked, they managed to figure out a way to raise a machine off the floor. This meant it could turn out larger components and the company could bid for better contracts. These are the kind of people you want in your team.

So look for these clues when interviewing:

- **Do they run their own mind or does someone do it for them?** You'll be listening for clues such as: 'My husband suggested I do this' or 'My mother says that I should' or 'My family were all engineers so that's how I ended up becoming one.' None of this is wrong in its own right but it will give you an indication as to whether this person runs their own mind or not.

- **Can they solve problems?** Do they think things through and try to find a solution? Or do they let someone else do it for them? You're listening for: 'When I get a difficult customer I believe it's best to let my manager deal with them.' Or alternatively: 'I had a real crisis on my hands so I considered what options I had and …'.

- **Are they fairly disciplined?** Is there structure in their life and work or do they just react to circumstances. You're listening for – 'Before I start a job I like to plan how I'm going to do it.'

- **Are they creative?** Do they look for new ways to do things? You're listening for: 'We always used to fill out reports in a certain way but I suggested to my manager a way that would save time.'

- **Can they arrange things?** Do they have the ability to organise themselves and others? You're listening for: 'One of the team was leaving so I organised a going away party.'

- **Do they think about their own performance?** Are they questioning themselves and thinking about how they could do better? You're listening for: 'I was really unhappy with my results so I decided to…'

We're coming to the questions you will ask at an interview. However, it's important to know and recognise what you're listening for.

Belief

Someone who has belief in themselves is going to be good for your team. If they don't then they'll be forever checking with you and often taking too much time to make a decision.

> *Someone who has belief in themselves is going to be good for your team.*

What you're looking for is:

- **Self-motivation?** Do they indicate that they are motivated from within or do they need external motivation? You're listening for: 'I always check with my manager before I do this job so that **we** can be sure there will be no mistakes.' Someone who is **not** self-motivated will also talk about '**We** did this' or '**We** like to treat customers...'. Someone who **is** self-motivated is more likely to say '**I** did this' or '**I** like to treat customers...'.

- **Do they have drive?** Is there something that drives them on, some sort of goal or ambition? You're listening for: 'I'd like to improve my ability to...' or 'My objective is to...'.

- **Do they want to achieve things?** You're listening for: 'I want to gain a qualification in...'.

- **Do they have values and ethics?** You're listening for: 'I believe that...' or 'I feel it is important to...'.

- **How do their beliefs and values impact on others?** You're listening for: 'I put this point to the other guys in the team and they agreed that...'.

Many people suffer from low self-esteem and have often had the belief knocked out of them. We considered this earlier when we looked at how belief was important to you as a manager. It's so easy to allow the people above and around you to kill your self-belief.

The people you employ may have been brought up in a work environment that knocked their self-belief. Your job is to identify any spark that is still there and think about how you can revive it.

Energy

Just as you need energy to do your job, so the person you employ will also need energy. You're looking for brain energy and body energy. That doesn't mean that you're looking for someone who can't sit still and wants to dash about all over the place. However, you're looking for someone with the mental and physical stamina to do the job. Look for:

> *You're looking for someone with the mental and physical stamina to do the job.*

- **How they spend their leisure time?** Do they have a sedentary lifestyle? Do they crash out in front of the TV every night or do they do other things? Do they read, play music or have other hobbies or interests?

- **Do they have an enquiring mind?** You're listening for evidence that they want to find out things.

- **Do they exercise?** Do they talk about going to the gym, swimming, cycling or jogging?

- **Are they overweight?** This is a bit of a tough one as current research tells us that 61 per cent of Americans are overweight or obese. Most adults in the UK are overweight and one in five is obese. Overweight people are more likely to suffer poor health and be off work. The National Audit office in the UK estimates that obesity accounts for 18 million days of sickness annually. However, you have to ask yourself if this potential team member has the energy to do the job and give you the outcomes you need.

- **Do they look or sound stressed?** Is there evidence that they allow situations to 'get' to them?

- **Do they seem calm and relaxed?** Do they look like they can handle whatever comes along?

We're not talking about the perfect physical and mental specimen here; we're just looking for someone who can take what the world hands out. Some people can do it better than others and these are the people you're looking for.

Rapport

There aren't many jobs nowadays where the ability to get on with others isn't important. I mentioned earlier about delivery drivers who spent more time with customers than anyone else in the company. Motor mechanics, telecom engineers, hotel housekeepers are all the types of jobs where in the past people were employed primarily for their technical ability and their skill to do the job. Even if someone has virtually no external customer contact, they probably have many internal customer contacts that they interact with every day.

Some colleagues and I recently completed extensive customer care training for a major UK bank. I'm pleased to say that every employee in that organisation attended the training. We worked with retail branch staff, head office admin people, computer engineers, printers, maintenance engineers and call centre sales people. This organisation realised that if they had good communications internally then they had a better chance of having good communications externally.

So when you're interviewing look for:

- **People who listen?** Do they look like they're listening and taking in what you say? Watch for that expression on their face that tells you they may just be waiting for you to finish so they can speak.

- **Do they ask questions?** I don't mean the standard interview questions that some book told them to ask. Do they have a genuine enquiring mind? Are they really interested in what they are getting into?

- **Good relationships.** You're listening for stories about how they built a relationship with a customer. How did they 'fit in' when they joined their existing team and how do they get on now? Don't accept good family relationships as evidence of their ability to build relationships in the workplace – it may not follow.

- **Empathy.** Do they put themselves in the other person's situation? You're listening for: 'I really felt for that person, I could understand their situation.'

- **Enthusiasm.** Do they demonstrate enthusiasm for situations in their work and personal life?

- **Persuasive.** Do they sound like they could persuade someone else to their point of view? You're listening for: 'This customer wanted the newer model but I demonstrated to her how the existing model met her needs.'

- **Take command.** Do they have the ability to take charge of a situation? You're listening for: 'This customer was really unhappy so I decided to organise a special delivery.'

You're looking and listening for any evidence that gives you an indication of how this person interacts with other people.

Courage

As I said earlier, the old-style manager doesn't encourage people to think and certainly doesn't look for courage as a job characteristic. They would more likely be looking for a subservient type of person who did what they were told without question. That's not what you want; you want someone who has the courage to act.

> *You want someone who has the courage to act.*

So look for:

- **A willingness to try**. Someone who's prepared to have a go, or in the words of Captain Kirk, 'To boldly go where no man has gone before.'

- **Mistakes.** You want someone who isn't afraid to make mistakes and is prepared to learn from them. You're listening for: 'I realised I'd made a mistake so I decided to…'

- **Assertiveness.** You don't want someone who is aggressive, but neither do you want someone who is non-assertive. You're looking for someone who has the courage of their convictions and who isn't afraid to make their point.

- **Overcoming resistance.** You're looking for someone who can deal with the challenges that work and life throws at us. Not someone who will respond aggressively, just someone who can deal with the challenges raised by customers and colleagues.

Consider all of the Five Factors of success when you come to interview someone. Obviously you're not looking for every characteristic in

> *Consider all of the Five Factors of Success when you come to interview someone.*

an applicant. However, they'll help you to focus your thoughts and identify the talents that you're looking for.

Think about your team

As you prepare to interview a new member for your team it may help you to think about the people you already have. What talents do they have that make them produce the outcomes? I know that this can sometimes be quite difficult, because I would try to identify what made my good guys good. It comes down to the skills you apply when spending time with your people (we're coming on to these in the next chapter). You have to spend time listening, observing what they do and using the thinking bit of your brain.

I had one particularly successful salesman who could really bring in the business. However, he certainly wasn't your stereotypical salesman type; he was kind of quiet and laid back. I watched him one day with a customer and it 'clicked' with me; he was the world's greatest listener and the customers loved it. He would ask the customer relevant questions, which he knew would take him where he wanted to go and then he'd listen intently. He didn't have to ask for the order – the customers asked *him* if it would be okay to place an order.

> *Find out what makes your good guys good and look for it in others.*

Find out what makes your good guys good and look for it in others.

BEFORE THE INTERVIEW

As well as all the factors we've considered previously, there are some other important things you need to think about before the interview.

Time

Devote a lot of time to the interview process. As a manager this is one of the most important jobs you'll ever have to do. Picking a new member for your team is a vitally important job, and if you don't take the time you could regret it later.

> *Picking a new member for your team is a vitally important job, and if you don't take the time you could regret it later.*

Do you remember the telesales team that I talked about in Chapter 2? How I took over an underperforming team from another manager? I was interviewing one day for new telesales agents and John the ex-manager was aware of what was going on. He let me know his thoughts: 'You've had that person in there for forty-five minutes,' he said. 'I used to get them in for an interview and made a decision whether to hire them or not in fifteen minutes, sometimes less.' He was incredulous when I informed him that, 'Yes, I'll interview for about forty-five minutes and I'll have them in again for another forty-five minutes before I make a decision.' Of course, as you'll remember, John had nothing but problems with this team.

It doesn't need to be forty-five minutes. It's possible that you could identify if this person has the talent you want (or not) within thirty minutes. However, I think fifteen minutes is a bit too quick.

Be prepared not to choose someone

Take your time and don't feel pressured to make a decision. If you don't find the person you want then start the selection process again. Some managers seem to believe that they need to pick some-

> *Take your time and don't feel pressured to make a decision.*

one out of the people they interview and pick the 'best of the bunch' – this is a recipe for disaster.

This is also where you'll need your courage as a manager because you may come under pressure from your boss to appoint someone. I've had a senior manager say to me, 'There must be someone in that group that you want to hire. Are you sure you've looked closely enough?' I even had one manager insist that I bring interviewees in again so that he could interview them. He rejected them all.

Plan ahead

Before the interview you will probably have a CV to study and the results of any screening process. You may even have the results of some kind of psychometric test. However, none of these have any relevance to the interview you're going to have with the applicant.

Some managers pore over the CV during the interview and spend time checking the facts with the applicant. That's not going to help you unearth the talents that this person needs to do the job. The Motivational Manager will use all the information he can to come to a decision about an applicant. However, to identify the talent to do the job is going to take some careful questioning during the interview. You may only need to prepare about four or five questions depending on what you want to find out.

THE INTERVIEW PROCESS

Relax the applicant

This is nigh-on impossible to do because almost anyone being interviewed for a job will feel nervous. However, don't make it harder for them by creating some kind of pressure chamber or interrogation room.

Be warm and friendly and welcoming. However, don't get into too much small talk or before long they'll be telling you all about their last vacation in Florida.

I can remember interviewing a guy called Steve for a sales engineer's job. As soon as he entered the room I could see he was a *big* guy, the kind of guy you're careful to shake hands with in case he crushes your fingers. He dropped himself down on the chair, sat back, broke the back of the chair and did a somersault onto the floor. I was trying not to laugh as I picked him up off the floor, his interview suit and his hair all disarranged and his tie twisted round his neck. I managed to get him into another chair and we carried on with the interview.

He was a real gentle giant of a guy and at a later stage I offered him the job; he went on to be very successful. Some months later when we were out seeing customers together he asked me, 'When I came for my interview and fell over the back of that chair, was that some kind of test to see how I'd act under pressure?' The poor guy believed that I'd loosened the chair back to see how he'd react to an involuntary backward somersault.

Set the scene

Let the applicant know that you want to find out if they have the talent to do the job you need. Make it clear that you will be asking some structured questions and that you want them to say how they feel and what they think. Explain that it could be different from any interview they've had before and that you want to make a decision that is best for both of you.

Make it clear that you'll allow time at the end of the interview for them to ask any questions they have. However, let them know that if they're invited back for a second interview then that would be the best time for them to ask questions.

This interview is where you will decide if this person has the talent to do the job; it's not where you talk about the duties involved, the benefits or the salary. You can get to all of that at a second interview. If they ask any questions about salary (if it hasn't already been made clear) then there's no reason not to tell them. In fact, I quite like people who want to know what they're getting paid.

The questions

Based on the talent you're looking for, you need to have prepared questions before the interview. **Do not** interview by the seat of your pants and ask questions as you think of them. You could then end up just having a 'chat' and you will never uncover the talent you're looking for.

You've heard all the stuff about open and closed questions; what you want in an interview is open questions that allow the person to go in various directions. You want them to reveal how they would respond if faced with the situations you know they'll encounter every day on the job.

Be careful that your questions don't give the applicant a clue as to the information you want. I once had an interviewer ask me, 'Are you the kind of person who likes to lie in their bed in the morning or do you like to get up and get going?' Strange but true!

You probably would never ask a question like that. However, you have to be careful of questions that 'telegraph' the answers you want. 'What do you enjoy most about being a maintenance engineer?' is going to get you answers like: 'I enjoy the challenge of solving customers' problems.' Yuck!

Or how about, 'How important do you believe accuracy is in reports?'. I'm not even going to comment on that one!

'Tell me about a time' questions are good

If you were looking for a customer service person who you wanted to build good relationships with your key accounts, then you might ask a question such as, 'Tell me about a time when you built a relationship with a customer.'

If the individual *is* good at building relationships then they'll immediately respond with a case history. If they ask you, 'What do you mean?' simply repeat the question. If you start to prompt them or put the question in a different way, then you're in danger of telegraphing the direction you want the applicant to take.

Listen for specifics

Some applicants will answer the above question with something like, 'I have good relationships with all my customers, it's difficult to give you a specific example.' The reason they say that is because they *don't have* a specific example. They may just be a 'processor of customers' and don't really build good relationships.

The good guys will tell you stories such as, 'I've dealt with Susan at the Acme Tool Company for the past two years. We didn't get on too well when I first made contact because we'd let her down on deliveries a couple of times. So I decided to set up a system whereby I'd contact Susan once a week and discuss the order situation with her. We get on really well now and she's even asked me to come and visit her company.'

When you start to hear stories like this you can listen for the factors you need for the job.

'**How do you feel**' questions are also good.

You might ask an applicant, 'How do you feel when a customer is angry about the service from your company?' You may get the response, 'It's no problem to me, I can handle it, water off a duck's back, I sort their problem out.'

If you were looking for someone with the talent to empathise with your customers, then you're not getting it here. The response you're looking for should be something like, 'I feel really uncomfortable for the customer when we don't get it right, I realise that it must be very frustrating for them. I listen carefully to what they have to say and make it clear that I do care about their situation and tell them what I'll do to resolve it.'

'What gives you great personal satisfaction?' is another good question

Every individual is different and what is personally satisfying for one may not be for another. I'm sure there are many jobs that you wouldn't think of applying for no matter how much they paid. I find it hard to understand what anyone would find satisfying in being an accountant or a dentist; however, many people do. Some people find it really satisfying to turn round a difficult customer or negotiate a loan. Finding out what an applicant finds satisfying will give you clues to their talents.

Keep thinking ...

The benefit of having structured questions prepared beforehand means that you don't need to be thinking about what to ask next. You can devote all of your time to listening for the information you need.

> *Having structured questions prepared beforehand means that you don't need to be thinking about what to ask next.*

It's also important to keep your thinking brain engaged: don't let your heart rule your head. If you were to hear, 'I hate customers who don't know what they want', don't think, 'It'll be okay, they probably don't mean that.' The thing is, they probably do and it may cause problems with their ability to build the customer relationships you need. The trick is to believe what the applicant says and don't put your own interpretation on the answer.

Remember what we said in Chapter 2 about not making people what they're not. Too often a manager will interview someone and realise that they may not quite have the talent they're looking for. The manager then thinks, 'It'll be all right. Once they've started in the job I'll train them or I'll sort them out.' You'll only be able to bring out a talent that's there in the first place, so you're going to have to be sure that it's there. Remember what I said about my piano lessons as a youngster; I just don't have the talent. You could probably teach me to play a piano but if you want me to play in your band, it'll be a total disaster.

As long as the applicant is talking and you're carefully listening and thinking then you're more likely to pick up the information you need.

... but listen to your 'gut'

I made the point in Chapter 2 about how difficult a manager's job is. Picking people for your team is one of the hardest things you'll have to do. Again, it's because people are so complex. However, if you can keep focused on the talents you're looking for then you'll minimise the risk of picking the wrong person. I've made the point about thinking and that's what you need to do to structure your questions. However, I've also made the point about listening to your intuition. If it doesn't feel right with a job applicant then don't employ them, it isn't worth the risk. If you think, 'This guy's a good maintenance engineer but his interpersonal skills leave a lot to be desired', don't employ him if he has to work closely with customers.

Keep your eyes open

Up until now we've been talking about asking questions and listening. However, it's also important to do some watching. I'm sure that you're aware of the importance of body language and the fact that it can often contradict what we hear.

Just imagine or even remember a situation where you met someone and they said, 'It's so good to see you, I'm so glad we met!' The only thing is – they don't look pleased to see you or

> *It's important to use your eyes as well as your ears when you're interviewing someone.*

glad you met. There's something about their manner that contradicts what they're saying. We tend to believe what we see rather than what we hear. That's why it's important to use your eyes as well as your ears when you're interviewing someone.

Here's a story about me not keeping my eyes open. Christine, the telesales manager, and I were interviewing Joyce for a telesales agent's job. Towards the end of the interview I asked Joyce if she had any more questions or if there was anything she wanted to say. She came back with, 'You're probably wondering why I've got two different shoes on.' She then went on to explain that she'd changed her shoes in the car and didn't realise till she came into the interview that she had slipped on two different but similar black shoes. I hadn't noticed a thing but Christine had spent the whole interview thinking, 'Why has this lady got two different shoes on?'

We had a bit of a laugh with the lady before she left. However, in our post-interview discussion, Christine and I both felt that this lady would have difficulty dealing with the customer situations that were part of the job. We felt from what she'd said that she was a little bit 'scatterbrained' and the incident with the different shoes only added to that conclusion.

You little liar

You have to accept the fact that job applicants will tell lies when they're being interviewed. Not necessarily big, bad black lies but maybe some

> *Job applicants will tell lies when they're being interviewed.*

little white ones. The little white ones are sometimes just a little bit of exaggeration. They might say something like, 'I was the most successful sales person in our team.' Now that may have been on a particular day last November and it isn't something you need to get too concerned about. What you do need to be concerned about, however, are people who say things about themselves that are blatantly untrue.

If you use the questioning techniques described earlier and you listen well, you'll pick up inconsistencies in what someone says. There are some people who are so good at telling lies that they could fool a lie detector machine while under the influence of a truth drug. However, the majority of people aren't that good at continually telling untruths. As you listen to the applicant you'll sometimes find yourself thinking, 'That's funny, they said a short while ago that they fully understood the xyz software, now they're saying something different.' So the message is still keep listening. However, keep watching for other signals.

She 'nose' you know

There are lots of good books on understanding body language and I suggest you have a look at one. However, it's not a very exact science and it's easy to misread the signals. For example, is this person scratching their nose because it's itchy, because they're telling a lie or because they're just nervous being inter-viewed? The trick is to match the body language with the response to a particular question. Say you had asked, 'Tell me about a time you negotiated a big order.' If the person keeps touching their nose as they tell you the story, it may be an indica-tion that they're making it up.

Apparently, and this has come out of research, your nose swells slightly if you tell a lie (and my nose isn't swelling as I write this). It's all to do with an increased blood flow to the nose which can cause it to grow or become itchy. So there's obviously some truth in the Pinocchio story.

Sometimes nose touching is also an attempt to cover the mouth and stop the lie coming out. Just think about children when they tell a porky pie. They tend to put their hand up to cover their mouth – it doesn't quite go away when we become adults.

The eyes have it

They say the eyes are 'the window to the soul' and they can certainly tell you a lot about what an applicant is thinking. We all know about people who look away appearing furtive or excessive blinking as a sign of nervousness. However, we can learn other things from the eyes.

Let's say you ask someone one of your 'Tell me about a time' questions. If their eyes flick up to their left as they tell the story, this means that they are accessing their visual memory. In other words, they're thinking about a real situation. If their eyes flick up to the right as they speak, then they're creating something in their mind. In other words, they're telling lies.

If you've never heard this stuff before then I know you'll be a bit sceptical. However, it's just one of the techniques being used by police and other interrogators. I suggest you observe some of the people you deal with in your personal and business life. Ask them about their trip to Hawaii and watch their eyes. I bet you see lots of flicks to the left. If their eyes are flicking to the right then maybe they didn't really go to Hawaii and spent their vacation in front of the TV. Try it – I've been doing it for years and it works.

I've said it before and I'll say it again: picking people for your team is one of the most important jobs you'll ever do. Use every bit of

> *Be as good an interviewer as you can be – good questions – good listening – good watching.*

information you can get your hands on, read the CV and study any psychometric test that's been done. However, be as good an interviewer as you can be – good questions – good listening – good watching.

4
Spend some quality time

I've already made the point in Chapter 1 that managing people *well* is a hard job. There are many managers who believe they manage well and then go on to tell you about the hassle they have with some of their people and how stressed it makes them feel. That to me is not what managing well is all about. Throughout this book I'm talking about managing people in a way that's easy for you and ensures you achieve your outcomes.

One of the reasons I said that a manager's job is tough is because every member of your team is different. Do you remember my story about driving the car – how every model is different? However, if you understand the particular car, know which buttons to push and the direction to steer it in, then life becomes much easier. So it's important to spend time getting to know the particular model you're dealing with – or in your case, the members of your team.

It's also an ongoing process because people change constantly and they're much more complex than any car will ever be. If you're married or have ever been in a long-term relationship then I bet there have been times when you've said, 'I just don't understand this person.' I was married for fifteen years and I knew my wife for five years before that. I was still finding out things about Elizabeth in year twenty that I never knew about her before.

If you want to make your job easy and achieve your outcomes then you need to get to know your people – you need to spend quality time with them. In Chapter 2 I talked about the Five Factors of Success. This is number four – Rapport. Successful people are good at it and it follows that successful managers are too. If you've forgotten what I said about it, take a look back at Chapter 2.

I've worked for several managers and the only thing that some of them knew about me was that I was male and I could breathe in and out. So I didn't think much of them either. I know you're not like that, but I'm also sure you're not spending the quality time you should be with your team.

WHY DO IT?

Let's look at some of the benefits of spending quality time with your people:

- You'll get to understand them better.

- You'll get to understand how they're handling the job.

- It will help you build a relationship with each individual.

- It will give them the impression that you care about them as individuals (a big motivator).

- It will show that you're there to help with problems.

- It encourages opinions and ideas to flow from them.

- It allows you to explain the company's mission.

- It gives them a feeling of being 'in on things' (another big motivator).

- It helps them get to know you.

- You will get an early warning of any problems, business or personal.

- It builds team spirit and morale.

- It gives you a chance to give them feedback on their performance (another big motivator).

- It gives them the chance to give you feedback on your performance (scary).

- It allows you to coach on the job, which helps them to learn and grow.

- And of course – it helps you to achieve your outcomes and minimise your stress.

Let's take a closer look at eight of these benefits of spending quality time:

Benefit 1 – You get to understand them better

One of my clients is an industrial equipment hire company. They have depots throughout the country and hire out all sorts of tools and equipment. The tools are stored at the depots where a team of engineers carries out the maintenance. One of these teams is supervised by a guy called Steve. Steve was a real 'problem child' at work, always complaining or whinging. He was a real headache for his boss, the General Manager, Bill. They always seemed to be arguing about something or other. One day Bill tells me, 'I'm sending Steve on your customer service course. I want you to sort him out.' As you'll appreciate, I don't run customer service courses to 'sort people out'.

Steve attended the course and gave us all his thoughts on why the company's service was so bad and why they were wasting their money on courses like this. Now you may wonder why they didn't get rid of Steve. However, even though he was so difficult to deal with, he did a pretty good job. Of course, the team that he was supervising always seemed to have problems as well.

I ran quite a few courses for this company and regularly came into contact with Steve in and around the office. He usually just gave me a grunt as we passed and gave the distinct impression that he didn't think much of me.

One day I was sitting waiting in the reception area to see Bill; Steve appeared in reception, gave his usual grunt and sat down; he was also waiting for a word with Bill. My natural reaction was to let Steve stew in his own juice. However, I decided to practise a bit of what I preach. 'How are you Steve?' I asked. 'How's that football team of yours doing in the league?' Now I knew that Steve was a big football fan and my interest and questions started him talking. I'm not a football expert but I knew enough to keep the conversation going. After a while we exhausted that topic so I asked him, 'Are you married Steve?' 'Yes, why?' Like no one had ever asked him that question before. 'Been married long?' 'Yes, twelve years.' 'Any children?' 'No, but Jo's pregnant at the moment.' He then went on to tell me how they both wanted children very much but they'd had lots of problems in trying to start a family.

I just expressed interest and understanding and kept listening.

When I eventually went into Bill's office I asked him, 'Did you know that Steve's wife is pregnant?' Bill gave me a disinterested response. I persevered. 'Seems like they've had a lot of problems.' 'So what?' was the reply, so we got down to business

From that day forward Steve and I had a different relationship. When we'd pass in the office or the yard it was always, 'How's it going Al?' I'd respond with a joking remark about his football team or sometimes just enquire how Jo was doing with the new baby. Steve was always going to be a difficult guy to deal with and I knew that we would never be best buddies. However, I do know that if I had been Steve's boss then we could have worked pretty well together. If Bill could only get this message, he could make both their lives much easier.

This story always reminds me of something Abraham Lincoln once said. 'I don't think I like that man, I must get to know him better.'

It's very easy for a manager to fall into the trap of condemning one of their team as a no-hoper or a problem child. It may turn out that this person shouldn't be on your team. However, you need to try the Abraham Lincoln theory first.

Of course, we're not just talking about difficult members of your team; we're talking about all of them and how important it is to understand them as individuals. It's important because it's important to them.

As Dr Phillip C. McGraw says in his book, *Life Strategies*: 'The number one need among all people is acceptance.'

> *Your team want to know that you accept them from a work point of view but they also want you to accept them just for who they are.*

Your team want to know that you accept them from a work point of view but they also want you to accept them just for who they are.

Find out as much as you can about your team; their background, where they're from, families, pets, hobbies, sports and their views on the world. Find out their philosophies and faiths, how they think and how they feel. Just think about it like any other relationship – what do you want to know about this person?

Now I'm not suggesting you sit around all day gazing into each other's eyes or spend half the night on the phone. I'm suggesting you do this over time and slowly but surely build up your understanding of each person. I also know that you're starting to get a bit nervous about this and might think it's prying. You're also thinking that your team members won't want you to get to know them that well. Let me reassure you – most of them will, if it's done discretely. And in a short while I'm going to give you some questions to ask.

Almost everyone wants to know that someone is genuinely and positively interested in them. They may not always give that impression by their demeanour, but trust me – they want to know you care; they want acceptance from you. If they know you care about them, then your relationship will be much more productive.

Benefit 2 – You find out how they're handling the job

As well as getting to know the members of your team on a human or personal basis, you need to get to know them on a business basis. How are they getting along with the job? And it's not a matter of asking, 'How's the job going?' If you ask that then you may get a list of complaints or you may just get, 'It's all going fine.'

In some ways it's better to get the complaints, because then you have a chance to do something about them or at least show you care. It's just like good customer service; you really need to know from customers who aren't happy so that you can put it right. Too many customers don't say anything to you and just moan to other people. Does that sound like any of your team?

I have a friend, Brian, who is General Manager for a small construction company. He always seems to have a high turnover of staff, particularly the people in the office. One day he tells me, 'Had to get rid of another girl today; totally useless and wasn't doing the job properly.' I started to ask him about how he hired people and about their initial and ongoing training.

'When they start on day one I put them with Susan; she's been here for years and she knows the ropes. Susan supervises them, keeps them right and lets me know if they haven't worked out.' 'But who's their manager?' I asked him. 'I am,' he says. 'Do you ever check to see if they understand the job?' was my next question. 'I ask them how they're doing and they usually say "Fine!" '

The analysis of this situation is this: Susan tells the new employee, 'Do this, do that; when a customer phones, fill in the form and if there's a problem just deal with it.'

Of course, what Brian needs to do is spend more time with the new employee; not hours and hours, just enough to really find out if she knows the job.

You can imagine what Brian is paying in recruitment costs, over and above the hassle of interviewing, starting new people and then getting rid of some of them. Spending a bit more time with new employees could reduce his costs and his stress.

You need to know how your team members are handling the job so you need to ask the right questions. Again, in a short while, I'll show you some questions to ask.

Benefit 3 – It helps you deal with problems

One of the main benefits of spending time with your team is that it lets them know you're there to help with problems. Of course, you're not there necessarily to solve their problems but to coach them to solve their problems (more of this in Chapter 8).

It also gives you an early warning of any personal or business problems that could occur. A team member might tell you about one of their children having a problem at school that could lead to something more serious. They might even indicate a problem in their marriage or relationship. You can see the storm clouds brewing or it may just be a squall, but one way or another you'll be ready.

> *Having regular contact with your team also prepares you for any potential business problems.*

Having regular contact with your team also prepares you for any potential business problems, such as failing to meet your target or product supply problems or anything else that will affect your outcomes.

Benefit 4 – Your team get to know you

Spending time with your team lets them get to know you. When I'm running a training course, particularly a two- or a five-day course, I'm often surprised by the participants' interest in me. Sometimes I think it's just polite conversation. However, most of the time that doesn't seem to be the case. They always want to know how old I am for some reason.

Your team will want to know about you at both a personal and business level. Again, that doesn't mean sharing your intimate thoughts but it's similar to the things you want to know about them. Even though team members don't ask you about yourself, tell them. Reveal bits and pieces about yourself over a period of time. Good professional speakers know this. They let their audiences know various things about themselves that show their idiosyncrasies or little mistakes they've made. What you're really saying is, 'I'm human, I'm like you, I experience the same situations.'

A lady approached me after one of my presentation skills seminars. She said, 'I was really interested when you said you were nervous before giving a speech; that made me feel so much better knowing you're just like me.'

> *Your team members want to know that 'you're just like them'.*

Your team members want to know that 'you're just like them'. This is not detrimental to your role as a manager or team leader – in fact, it enhances it.

Benefit 5 – You have the opportunity to give them feedback and coach them

This is one of the most important things the Motivational Manager can do. This is your opportunity to tell them the things that you **do** like about their performance and also the things you **don't** like. Too often managers leave feedback until a performance review and these are often only once or twice a year.

When managers see things they don't like they often put off speaking to the team member about it until things become really serious. And commenting on things they do like isn't generally done often enough.

When you spend time with your team and see things you don't like, it gives you an ideal opportunity to coach them on the job.

The whole aspect of feedback and coaching is so important that we're going to look at it in much greater detail in Chapter 5.

Benefit 6 – They have the opportunity to give you feedback

Now this may make you feel a bit nervous and it certainly can be scary when you're not used to it, but it is very motivational. If you create a

> *If you create a healthy open environment in your team then they should feel comfortable giving feedback to you.*

healthy open environment in your team then they should feel

comfortable giving feedback to you. It may not always be what you want to hear but it can certainly improve your relationship with them.

Benefit 7 – It encourages opinions and ideas to flow from the team

It will often be the case that members of your team have positive suggestions that will benefit the team, the business and you. However, they may not always be willing to seek you out and tell you about them. Perhaps they may feel foolish or embarrassed in front of their colleagues. If you're spending time with them, this is the ideal opportunity for them to give you their thoughts. Of course, you sometimes have to dig this out and encourage it.

Not all of their ideas will be successfully implemented. However, encouraging ideas builds the team member's confidence in you and the organisation and it's good for morale.

Benefit 8 – It allows you to explain the company's mission and the team's role in this

When you spend time with each individual it gives you the opportunity to explain how the business is going and how the team is performing. This is often done at a team brief and that's okay. However, in a one-to-one situation you can discuss in more depth and encourage ideas and feedback from them as described above. One of the biggest motivators for people at work is a feeling of being 'in on things'. People at work want to know what's going on and they want to feel involved. We'll look at this closer in Chapter 9.

CHALLENGES TO TEAM QUALITY TIME

There are many benefits in spending quality time with your team members. However, like with many other things in this world, there are challenges.

- Your team feel uncomfortable.

- They think they're going to get a reprimand.

- They think your doing it just because you have to.

- You don't feel comfortable.

- You don't want to be seen as prying.

- It's seen as checking up.

- You don't want to handle personal issues.

- You don't have the answer to business problems.

- The team works at different locations.

- You don't have the time.

- You don't see the benefits.

Let's look at these challenges in detail.

Challenge 1 – They feel uncomfortable

Some people may feel uncomfortable when you sit down and spend time with them, particularly if they're not used to it. They might not be used to you or perhaps a previous manager didn't do it either. It's often the case

> *It's often the case that people are uncomfortable because they associate their manager sitting down with them as a prelude to a reprimand.*

that people are uncomfortable because they associate their manager sitting down with them as a prelude to a reprimand.

As Kenneth Blanchard and Spencer Johnson say in their book, *The One-Minute Manager*, 'Catch people doing something right.'

Too many managers think that their job is to catch people doing something wrong.

Do you remember how I talked in Chapter 1 about managers who thought their job was to check up on what their people were doing and 'sort things' as required? Many employees today feel that's still the situation. If a manager comes close to you then they're checking up. If you've got that culture among your team members, then you've got to change it.

Think of it this way: are you the kind of manager who spends time with your team to find out **what** they're doing or to find out **how** they're doing? Make sure it's the latter.

Some of your people may even be a bit scared of you, particularly when they first join the team. You may think that you're much too nice a person; how could anybody be scared of little old you? However, I used to think that also.

One day I was discussing a new salesman with John, one of the more experienced guys. 'Young Patrick's scared of you,' he said. 'Don't be ridiculous,' was my reply. 'What have I ever done to make him scared of me, I'm always really nice to him.' 'Well he is scared of you and just wants to please you,' said John. This was something that really made me think because there was no way I wanted any of my team to be scared of me. Once I was aware of it I took more care in my dealings with Patrick and our working relationship worked out okay.

Always be aware of the impact you're having on your people.

So always be aware of the impact you're having on your people; you may think that you're the nicest, most reasonable person in the world but how do they see it? Sadly, there are some managers who quite like the fact that their people are a bit scared of them and they see it as a positive situation. These are also the managers who spend a lot of time recruiting new people.

I can remember times when I've taken over a new team. I've had many strange looks and defensive body language when I've stopped to have a chat with some of the team.

Some field sales people would get extremely uncomfortable when I told them I'd be spending some time with them visiting customers. However, I realised that I was getting it right when at a later date a sales person would ask, 'When are you coming out with me again, Alan, to see some customers?'

There are always going to be members of your team who are really keen to spend time with you and others who are less so. However, you must spend time with everyone – more with some and less with others. If you do it right (and I'm about to show you how), then your people will start to get used to it and start to see the benefits to themselves.

Challenge 2 – You're doing it because you have to

When you start spending more quality time with your people, they sometimes think you're only doing it because you have to. This often happens when managers come back from a course. Team members think, 'Here we go again, another new management theory that means nothing to us.' Again, it's important to persevere and show your team that there are benefits for them.

A manager who attended one of my seminars returned to work and called one of his team on the phone who worked at another location. 'I'll come down and see you this week instead of you bringing the reports to me,' he told her. (He had suddenly realised that he never did this and it would be a good idea to visit his team member 'on the job'.) 'What do you want to do that for? You never do that,' was her incredulous reply. Sadly, the manager backed down. 'Okay, you just come and see me as usual,' he replied. This was a missed opportunity for this manager to speak with the team member on her territory, to show that he cared enough to get out of his office to go and see her.

Challenge 3 – You don't feel comfortable

A big challenge for many managers in spending time with their people is the fact that they don't feel comfortable. Most managers are okay when it comes to communicating instructions to their team or the usual 'How's the job going?' They are often not so comfortable when it comes to asking personal questions or delving into job performance a bit more.

They are terrified of being perceived as prying. They are also concerned that someone might say something that they have difficulty in dealing with. Responses like 'My husband has cancer' or 'My wife is leaving me for another man' can be difficult for any manager to handle. However, that's no reason for a manager to run away from asking the question.

Do you remember the Fifth Factor of Success – Courage? As I said at the time, a manager needs lots of it if they want to be successful and often it's just the courage to ask the question.

Challenge 4 – You don't have the answer to business problems

Some managers don't spend too much time with people because they're concerned they don't know how to answer the responses and comments that may come up. Questions such as 'How's the job going?' can result in a whole cacophony of moans and groans. 'Why are we being asked to do this? What's happening to the company? These targets are ridiculous.'

If these questions come up then they have to be dealt with. You're not always going to be able to give people the answers they're looking for. However, there are things you can do. Stay with me on this.

Challenge 5 – Team members at different locations

Some managers have teams that are spread all over the country. The obvious answer is to get out and see them as often as you can. However, I accept this isn't always easy. I've managed teams who were spread over the country and I appreciate the challenge it creates. Of course, there is always the telephone and in these days of mobile phones it is much easier to keep in touch. The new video mobile phones that are coming onto the market will also help the communications you have with your remote team members.

Challenge 6 – You don't have the time

Lack of time is one of the main reasons cited by managers for not spending time with their people. This is a bit of a red herring. A manager will say that they don't have the time to spend with their people mainly because they don't see the value in it.

Can you imagine a top sports coach saying that he doesn't have much time to spend with his team? I don't think that team will win the championship!

This book is about achieving your outcomes and making life easier for you. If you spend more quality time with your people then that's what will happen. All of us can find that bit more time. Remember what I said about successful managers – they run their own minds and they don't let anyone else do it for them.

I know the challenges you face particularly with your own manager. I've been about to leave the office to visit one of my team at another location. My boss stops me: 'I need to talk to you Alan. Can you come into my office?' I'm sure you've been in this situation or something similar; your boss is making demands on you that keep you from working with your team.

It's back to what I said about courage. You need to communicate to your manager that what you're doing is for the good of the team and ultimately the good of the business. Ask the boss if you can reschedule the meeting; as I'm sure you've experienced, these 'meetings' with the boss are often not about anything too important. In the situation above I suggested to my boss that we could talk on the phone as I drove to meet my team member. I let the boss know that this visit was important to the success of the team and would contribute to an increase in sales. What you're trying to get across is that if you 'go into the boss's office' it is detrimental to the success of the business. As

> *You don't win them all but the Motivational Manager never gives up.*

I've said before, you don't win them all but the Motivational Manager never gives up.

Before we look at all the ins and outs of spending quality time with the members of your team, I want you to consider a factor that is really important to human beings.

ACKNOWLEDGEMENT

Acknowledgement is about recognition or attention from another person. It can be physical, such as a pat on the back, a touch or a handshake. It can also be psychological, such as a word of praise, a compliment, even a 'hello'. It can even be just time spent with the person.

Physical and psychological attentions are absolutely vital to human beings. We all need them and we need them every day. However, it must be said that each human being has a different level of need for acknowledgement.

If you looked at it on a scale of 0 to 100 then there are a small number of people who'd be low on the scale. These are the people who cut themselves off from others, the hermits among us. The majority of people, however, are pretty far up that scale.

The need for acknowledgement is something that's programmed into us. Babies and children have a huge need for physical acknowledgement. You can see that demonstrated by the way they reach out for you, how they want to be held and cuddled.

Research has shown that infants who are denied this physical acknowledgement can suffer both in their physical and emotional growth.

As children develop their use of language, they start to need psychological attention as well. I'm sure you've experienced children coming to you with something they've drawn or made, looking for your praise.

As we grow into adulthood we become more sophisticated; however, our need for acknowledgement doesn't go away – we just seek it in a different way.

We send out all sorts of signals just to get acknowledgement.

We 'casually' mention some achievement: 'I've managed to reduce my golf handicap,' 'My boss has asked me to take on more responsibility' or 'Our child has just passed her exams.'

We take other actions to meet our need for acknowledgement. Do you remember the TV programme *Cheers* about the regular customers in a Boston bar? The show's signature theme had a line in it which went something like, 'Everybody goes where everybody knows your name!' The characters in *Cheers* don't just go to Cheers for a drink; they know that when they walk in the door someone, probably the person behind the bar, will acknowledge them.

I was speaking to a participant on one of my seminars and he was telling me all about his role as president of his local fishing club. All the things he had to do, the newsletter to write, the competitions to organise and the meetings to attend. I asked him if he got paid for it. 'Oh no,' was the reply. 'I do it because I like it.'

Of course he does it because he likes it, and no doubt it's a lot of work and takes up lots of his time. However, the acknowledgement he receives from this is massive.

I've known elderly parents who exaggerate illness just to get their family to visit and spend time with them.

A human's need for acknowledgement is so strong that they will sometimes behave badly to get that acknowledgement. I'm sure you're aware of children who behave badly in school just to get attention – well, adults do it too. That person in your team, who gives you all sorts of problems that are often difficult to understand, may just be seeking acknowledgement. We'll look at this a bit closer when we come on to dealing with problems in Chapter 8.

Your team members need acknowledgement and spending quality time with them is the way to do it. Just to be clear – acknowledgement isn't just about praising people; it's about spending time listening to and speaking with them. Let's take a closer look at how you spend quality time with your team.

> *Acknowledgement isn't just about praising people; it's about spending time listening to and speaking with them.*

HOW TO DO IT

1. Do it regularly

I can't tell you what regularly is for you but I can tell you that it isn't once a year or once a month. If you're managing a team, then I believe you should be speaking to your people every day or every other day either face to face or on the telephone. In the case of people who work at remote locations then there needs to be a lot more time spent on the phone with your team.

On a recent customer service seminar for a telecommunications company I asked one of the participants, 'What's the name of your manager?' I thought I might have met him on another seminar. Would you believe it? This man couldn't remember his manager's name! 'He's only been with us a few months,' he said, 'and I don't see much of him. I think his name's Dave something or other.'

It may be tempting to regard the team member here as not very bright but I believe it's the manager's fault. It doesn't matter whether he's a new manager or not, one of his first jobs should have been to really get to know his team.

Whether you work in an office with your team or they're spread around the country, it's absolutely vital to spend regular quality time with them.

2. Don't sneak up

If you work with your team in an office, don't sneak up from behind one of your team and plonk yourself down on a chair. Approach face on and ask if it's okay to interrupt: 'Is this a good time?' or 'Are you okay to speak at the moment?' It's the same with the phone; check that it's okay to talk before you launch into whatever it is you want to say. Too many managers seem to think that their needs take preference over anything else – 'I'm the manager and if I want to talk, we talk.' If that's you then please change your program. If you check that it's okay to speak then your people will respect your courtesy.

If you have a team working in different parts of the country, give each person plenty of warning that you want to visit and spend time with them. If you phone up and say, 'I'm seeing you tomorrow, meet me at such and such', you'll only give the impression that you're 'checking up'.

3. Don't be scary

Smile, look positive and be positive. It's not a good idea to start your conversation with, 'Pity about the

> *Smile, look positive and be positive.*

layoffs at the other office, hope it doesn't happen here.' Or even, 'It's really lousy weather today, isn't it?' The conversation can only go downhill from there.

It's not about being all 'rah-rah' and super-positive all the time; that probably isn't your style anyway. It's just about not being negative and miserable. You're looking to inspire your team, stimulate them and – hopefully – brighten their day!

It's also a good idea to be aware of how you look. There's a tendency nowadays for people working in offices to 'dress down'. The thinking being, 'I'm sitting here working at my computer and speaking on the telephone; the customers can't see me so it doesn't matter how I'm dressed.' Well I think it does.

Some years ago I appointed a new manager to a customer service team that I was responsible for. The customer service team tended to be very relaxed as far as their dress sense was concerned; jeans, tennis shoes, etc. However, Patricia, the new manager, was a very smart dresser. I don't mean over-the-top inappropriate dress, just smart and modern. After a few weeks of Patricia being in charge, I started to notice a difference in this team; they started to dress smarter. I know that Patricia didn't say anything to them; they just started to dress a bit more like her. Funnily enough, their approach and attitude also started to get a bit smarter.

If you approach your team looking like an unmade bed then think for a moment about the effect it has on them. If you look sloppy then you act sloppy and your team will be sloppy.

> *If you look sloppy then you act sloppy and your team will be sloppy.*

The time you spend with your team will have an effect on them. They need to feel better, brighter and sharper when you leave them than before you spoke to them.

4. Mix the human and the business

There are two levels on which you speak with your team; the human or personal level and the business level. It's always best to open any conversation on the human level. I once worked for a manager who was excellent at this.

Stuart was the Director of Sales and I was a regional manager with six sales engineers. Stuart was my boss and he was located about four hundred miles from me so I didn't see him too often. However, we did have regular contact by phone. He would always open any call on the human level. He would come on the phone with something like, 'Hi Alan, I trust you're well?' He then might say, 'How's Elizabeth? Did she get that new job she went after?' Stuart always seemed to remember these things. We would then have a short conversation about that and then he'd get down to business. Sometimes the business bit wasn't always something I wanted to hear: 'Your sales figures are slipping Alan, what are you doing about it?' or 'Your team's reporting is not up to scratch; I need you to do something about it.'

Stuart was no soft touch and his approach was never 'touchy feely'. However, I always felt that Stuart cared about me as an individual and I would always work well for Stuart.

Of course, this doesn't mean to say that every time you speak with your team that you launch into some personal discussion. Opening on a human level can take only a couple of words. And before I give you some examples – **you have to be genuine!**

Your team will know whether you mean something or not. I think most of us, by now, are aware of the importance of tone of voice and body language when we communicate. If you're not aware then just think of a time when somebody said something to you and it didn't sound as if they really meant it. 'Did you have a good weekend?' or 'I hope you enjoyed your vacation.' I'm sure you've found yourself thinking, 'You don't really mean that.'

So if you say something on the human level to one of your team, make sure you mean it or don't bother saying it. Just in case you're struggling, here are some things you could say.

- What did you think of Florida?

- How did the children (and use their names) enjoy Disney?

- I thought your team played really well last night.

- I like that tie.

- That's a really smart suit.

- You're looking well.

- I like your new glasses.

Also bring up things you've remembered: 'Did Dave pass his college exams?' or 'How's your husband's (use his name) new job?'

Americans are not usually shy about saying this kind of stuff. Europeans and Australians find it a bit more difficult. I've had British people on seminars who'll tell me, 'I'm not American; I don't like all that personal stuff.' Ironically, they'll then go on to tell me about visits to the US and how they liked the friendliness and warmth of the people. They'll admit, when pressed, that they really quite like it when someone pays them a compliment or makes a positive comment about them.

It's all back to what I said earlier about acknowledgement; human beings need and want it. Your team need and want it and it doesn't take much time to make a human comment. It's vital to your success as a Motivational Manager.

I said earlier about asking permission to speak to a team member. If you open a conversation with one of your team by saying, 'Is it okay to talk right now?' then you're using a human response. The message to the team member is, 'I value and respect you.'

Business questions or statements that could follow on from the human part of the conversation include:

- What challenges are you facing at present (don't use the word 'problems')?

- How can I help you do your job better?

- Do you see any challenges coming up for us?

- What figures do you have in relation to your target?

- I liked the way you handled that difficult customer this morning.

- That was a good suggestion you made about the reporting system.

This is the time to give your team members feedback on their performance, be it good or not so good. In the next chapter we'll look in detail at how to do it.

DEALING WITH CONCERNS

One of the challenges I mentioned earlier was about how to deal with your team members, concerns. When you spend time with your people then it's inevitable that that you'll hear about their concerns and problems. These could be on a human level. However, they're more likely to be on a business level. Whether it's a human or a business problem, the same rules apply. You're now thinking, 'I thought we weren't to use the word "problem".' We use the word 'challenge', never 'problem', when talking to a team member or a customer. Our team members are our internal customers and we deal with their issues in exactly the same way we'd deal with external customers.

> *Our team members are our internal customers and we deal with their issues in exactly the same way we'd deal with external customers.*

We are going to look much closer at problem solving in Chapter 8. However, for the moment let's look at how you can deal with concerns as you spend time with members of your team.

Fourteen steps for success in dealing with concerns

1. Don't get hooked

Remember the first Factor of Success – Mind Control. Don't react to a concern. It's very easy to react with, 'Here we go again, the same old moans and groans. They're always on about this and there's nothing I can do.' If you react this way, then it'll show on your face and in your tone of voice. The team member then thinks, 'What's the point? He's not interested in my problems. Why should I bother?'

Get into 'thinking mode' and stay out of it emotionally. Concentrate on listening non-defensively and actively. If the team member makes disparaging and emotional remarks – **don't rise to the bait**.

2. Listen – listen – listen

Look and sound like you're listening. When face to face you need to look interested, nod your head and keep good eye contact. Over the phone you need to make the occasional 'Uh-huh – I see.'

I've seen managers, when faced with a problem from a team member, start to do something else, like work on the computer. I've heard managers say, 'It's okay, I can do two things at once, I can listen to you and work on the computer.' Maybe you can, but the message your team member gets is, 'My problem isn't that important, my manager just isn't interested.'

> *When you're spending time with your people you need to give them your full attention.*

When you're spending time with your people you need to give them your full attention. You need to look them in the eye, concentrate on them and make them feel that what they say is important and deserves your attention.

3. Write it down

As well as looking interested in your team member's concern, it's a good idea to write it down. I've fallen into the trap of thinking, 'I'll remember that when I get back to the office and I'll check on it.' However, one person I was with said, 'You won't do anything about that Alan because you won't remember it.' From that point on I wrote things down.

4. Repeat back

It's also a good idea to paraphrase what the team member has said to ensure your understanding and let them know you've been listening.

5. Use names

It may seem like a simple thing but it's very important. You could say in response to a concern, 'I'll speak to the accounts department about that.' It would be far better to say, 'I'll speak to the accounts department about that Susan, thank you for bringing it to my attention.' That's a much better way for a Motivational Manager to respond.

A person's name is one of the warmest sounds they ever hear. Hearing it says, 'I recognise you as an individual.' However, I suggest you don't overdo it as it may come across as patronising.

6. Take ownership

As I said earlier, this is the same as dealing with an external customer. Your team members do not want to hear you say, 'That's nothing to do with me, that's the sales department's fault.' **Do not** blame someone or something else. It may **be** the responsibility of the sales department but it needs to be explained in a logical and factual way.

7. Watch out for people's egos

If your team member is really wound up about something, let them get it off their chest. Don't interrupt and don't argue. Don't jump in with solutions and try to solve the problem there and then. And for goodness sake, don't say, 'Calm down.'

8. See it from their point of view

You might find it hard to understand what they're on about. However, put yourself in their shoes. If you were doing their job every day, how would you feel? You might even think that their concern is something fairly trivial and think, 'What's the big deal? I'll fix it right away.' It **is** a big deal for the team member and they want you to appreciate it.

You don't necessarily need to agree with them. However you **do** need to accept the fact that it's a problem for them.

9. Be very aware of your body language and voice tone

As I mentioned earlier, we often exacerbate a situation without realising it. Our tone of voice and our body language can often contradict what we're saying. We may be saying 'sorry' but our tone and our body language may be communicating our frustration and annoyance. People listen with their eyes and will set greater credence on how you say something rather than what you say.

It's also important to use a warm tone of voice when dealing with a team member's problem. This doesn't mean being 'nicey-nicey' or behaving in a non-assertive manner. It's about showing that you're interested in what they're saying and that you care.

10. Words to avoid

We've looked at how tone of voice and body language can cause problems to get worse. Using the wrong words can also cause problems. There are certain 'trigger' words that cause people to become more difficult, especially in emotionally charged situations, and they should be avoided. These include:

- **Have to** – as in 'You'll have to speak to the sales department yourself.'

- **I can't or You can't** – as in 'I can't do anything about that' or 'You can't do that.'

- **I'll try** – as in 'I'll try to speak to the finance department today.'

- **But** – as in 'I agree with what you're saying but...'

- **Sorry** – as in 'I'm sorry about that.'

'What **do** I say?', I hear you cry.

Instead of 'have to', which are very controlling words, why not try 'John, are you willing to...' or just a straight 'John, will you...'?

'Can't' can be replaced with, 'I'm unable to because…'.

'I'll try', which is pretty wishy-washy, can be replaced with something more honest: 'This is what I can do, Mary' or 'This is what I'm unable to do.'

'But' is a word that contradicts what was said before it. Replace it with 'and' or 'however' (which is a soft 'but'). Instead of saying 'but' you could leave it out altogether. For example, instead of 'I agree with what you're saying but I cant help you', use 'I agree with what you're saying. The reason I'm unable to help you is…'.

The answer to the team member could still be 'no'. However, choosing your words more carefully will have a more positive effect on how he or she reacts and ultimately responds to you.

'Sorry' is one of the words to avoid because it is so overused and has lost its value. Think of the number

> *'Sorry' is one of the words to avoid because it is so overused.*

of times you've complained or commented about something and you hear 'Sorry about that.' If you're going to use the 'sorry' word then you need to use it as part of a whole sentence: 'Susan, I'm sorry you've been receiving so many complaints.'

Sometimes it's appropriate to use the word 'apologise' instead of 'sorry.' 'Linda, I apologise for not getting you that information sooner.'

There are other things you can say instead of 'sorry'. You can empathise.

11. Deal with their feelings, then deal with their problem

Using empathy is a very effective way of dealing with a person's feelings. Empathy isn't about agreement, only acceptance of what the team member is saying and feeling. Basically, the message is 'I understand how you feel'. This really has to be a genuine response. The person will realise if you're insincere and they'll feel patronised.

Examples of empathy are – 'Chris, I can understand that you're angry' or 'I see what you mean.' Again, these responses need to be genuine.

12. Build rapport

Sometimes it's useful to add another phrase to the empathy response, including yourself in the picture: 'I can understand how you feel Colin, I don't like that either when it happens to me.' This has the effect of getting on the team member's side and builds rapport.

Some people get concerned when using this response. They believe it will lead to 'Well why don't you do something about it then?' The majority of your team won't respond this way if they realise that you are a reasonable and caring person. If they do, then continue empathising and tell the individual what you'll do about the situation.

13. Under-promise – over-deliver

Whatever way you respond to a team member's problem, do not make a rod for your own back. It's often tempting in a difficult situation to make promises that are difficult to keep. We say things like, 'I'll get this sorted this afternoon Paul and I'll phone you back.' It may be extremely difficult to get it sorted 'this afternoon'. Far better to say, 'I'll get this sorted by tomorrow afternoon Paul.' Then phone Paul back the same afternoon or early the next morning and he'll think you're great.

14. You don't win them all

Remember, everyone gets a little mad from time to time and you won't always be able to placate or resolve your team member's problem – there's no magic formula. However, the majority of people are reasonable people (let's face it – you picked them) and if you treat them as such, then they're more likely to respond in a positive manner.

CONCLUSION

Spending quality time with your children, your wife, husband or partner is something you know you need to do if you want a happy and satisfying personal life. Spending quality time with your team members will give you a happy and satisfying business life.

When you spend time with your people, one of the most important things you can do is give them feedback. Let's look at how to do it.

5
Two types of feedback

HOW DO YOU FEEL ABOUT FEEDBACK?

Someone once said – 'Feedback is the breakfast of champions.'
Personally, I think that pancakes, crispy bacon and maple syrup
are the breakfast of champions. However, there's no doubt that
giving your team members feedback is absolutely vital to ensure
a motivated team who'll deliver
results. In Chapter 9 we'll take a
close look at what really motivates
people at work; however, one of the
top three factors is feedback.

> *Giving your team members
> feedback is absolutely vital to
> ensure a motivated team who'll
> deliver results.*

The majority of people want to know how they're doing at work.
They want to know when they're doing well and they want to
know when they could be doing better. There are a small minority of people who don't want feedback at all; but let's face it, you
don't want these people on your team anyway.

Okay, so I'll accept the fact that many people don't want to hear
bad things about their job performance. However, it depends on
how they hear the bad news that will affect their motivation at
work. I'm sure that you'd want to know if you were doing your
job okay; I know I would.

I used to run seminars on behalf of an American training company. Every so often they would send a senior training manager
to sit in on my seminars for a day or two and give me feedback.
Inevitably, from time to time, I might conduct part of the seminar
in a manner not quite in line with the way this training company

wanted it done. When it came to giving me feedback I was left in no doubt that they wanted it done in a particular way. Of course the training manager also told me what she did like about my way of running the seminar.

At the end of these feedback sessions I can always remember feeling good about myself. I was receiving feedback that confirmed what I was doing well and also some productive feedback that enabled me to do even better in the future.

Like many people, I can be very sensitive to negative feedback. At the end of any seminar or workshop I scan the feedback forms looking for any comment that would dare to suggest that I hadn't done a good job.

Remember what I said in Chapter 2 about thinking and not reacting? Well I've learned to practise what I preach. It's easy for me to look at negative feedback on the forms and say 'You can't please all the people all the time' or 'Who cares?' or 'What do they know?'. I try to keep an open mind and **think** about what's being said on the feedback forms. Is it something I should do something about? If this person didn't like something that I said, maybe there were others who felt the same way but didn't make any comment? All I want to do in my job is be the best that I can be, so it's important to listen to what my 'customers' have to say.

HOW DOES EVERYONE ELSE FEEL?

We all feel differently about feedback because we *are* all different. Some people love it, others are okay with it and others just hate it.

I'm sure that you have people on your team who always want to know how they're doing. They come and speak to you and show what they're doing. 'Is this okay boss, am I doing this right?' They are constantly looking for reassurance that they're doing the right thing. Then you'll have others on your team who never come and speak to you and get most uncomfortable whether you're giving them the good news or the bad.

I used to manage teams of field sales people and a lot of our conversations would be by telephone in the course of the working day. I also used to receive phone calls at home in the evening, usually about something I needed to be kept up to date on. However, there were always a couple of people on the team who would phone much more than others. 'Just wanted to let you know what happened with this customer today Alan' or 'just thought I'd update you on my figures.' Often it was information that was surplus to requirements but it was just that person's way of getting some feedback. They weren't necessarily looking for praise; they just needed to know that they were doing okay. It all ties in with the acknowledgement that we looked at earlier.

There were others in the team that I hardly ever heard from except when I phoned them or went to see them.

But let's think about you for a moment. You might be the kind of person who is comfortable with lots of feedback or maybe you'd prefer it in much smaller doses. The important point is this: the way you feel about receiving feedback could affect the way you give it to your team.

> *The way you feel about receiving feedback could affect the way you give it to your team.*

Managers who are happy to receive feedback are usually happy to give it to their team members because they believe their entire team feel the same as they do.

And of course, if you look at it the other way round, managers less comfortable with feedback tend to believe that their team feel the same way. This is often the biggest danger because many managers don't receive feedback from their manager and subconsciously feel, 'Why should I give feedback to my guys when I don't get it?'

Whether you receive feedback or not; whether you feel uncomfortable giving it or not – you still need to do it for your people. Just be aware that they're all different individuals and they might react in different ways. Almost everyone wants feedback – how much is just a matter of degree.

KEEP IT SIMPLE

Before we get into the different kinds of feedback and how we do it, I just want to be clear on a few points.

The feedback I'm talking about here isn't some sort of formalised appraisal that takes place with our team members every month or every six months or once a year. This feedback happens continually and it happens when you see or hear something you want to give feedback on. The trick is – keep it simple. If you see or hear something you **do** like, you tell the team member about it. If you see or hear something you **don't** like or feel could be done better, you tell the team member about it and you coach them.

CONFIRMING FEEDBACK

This is about giving the good news. It's about confirming to your team member that you approve of whatever it is you've seen them do or heard them say. It's a compliment or a thank you.

It also seems to be something that some managers have great difficulty with. They take the attitude 'Why tell people that you're pleased with them when they're only doing what they're paid to do in the first place.' A great deal of this attitude stems from what we said in Chapter 1, about managers having to be big and tough and macho. And managers don't do all that touchy-feely stuff; saying thank you is for wimps.

If you still feel a bit like that, think for a moment about how you felt when a manager gave you a genuine compliment or a thank you for a job well done. (Hopefully you can remember a time.) I bet you felt pretty good and probably motivated to do even better. I'm also sure you didn't think your boss was a big softy or that he lacked courage; probably the opposite.

Motivational Managers realise that almost every member of their team reacts positively to Confirming feedback. The team members feel better

> *Motivational Managers realise that almost every member of their team reacts positively to Confirming feedback.*

about themselves and they feel motivated to repeat the behaviour. There is a saying that goes, 'You get more of what you reward.'

Michael LeBoeuf tells this fable in his book *The Greatest Management Principle in the World*:

> A man went fishing one day. He looked over the side of his boat and saw a snake with a frog in its mouth. Feeling sorry for the frog, he reached down, gently took the frog from the snake and set the frog free. But then he felt sorry for the snake. He looked around the boat, but he had no food. All he had was a bottle of whisky; so he opened the bottle and gave the snake a few shots. The snake want off happy, the frog was happy and the man was happy to have performed such a good deed. He thought everything was fine until about ten minutes passed and he heard something knock against the side of the boat. With stunned disbelief, the fisherman looked down and saw the snake was back with two frogs!

I was setting up the room for a two-day training seminar in a hotel recently. The General Manager of the hotel happened to be passing and came into the room. He introduced himself: 'Good morning Mr Fairweather, my name is Tom Mitchell and I'm the General Manager. Is everything okay with your room and are you being looked after?' I was very pleased with his approach and I mentioned it to the Conference Manager later in the day. I asked him to speak to the General Manager: 'Please tell Mr Mitchell that I really liked the way he came into the room this morning, introduced himself to me and enquired if everything was okay. He made me feel like a special customer.'

The next morning as I was getting ready to start, the General Manager appeared again. 'Everything all right Mr Fairweather?' was his enquiry. Now I know that this manager doesn't go round all the meeting rooms every morning enquiring if everything is okay. I was just getting a bit more of 'what I had rewarded'.

So if you tell one of your team that you like the way they have completed some aspect of their work, you'll find that they continue to do that work in the same way or probably even better.

You've got to be genuine

Sometimes on a seminar, I ask the group, 'Who likes receiving compliments?' Often only a minority will put up their hand. I then ask, 'Who likes receiving a *genuine* compliment?' This time almost everyone puts up their hand. People often feel that a compliment isn't really meant and they sometimes feel a bit patronised. That's why it's important that your Confirming feedback *is* genuine and it sounds genuine. Don't say it if you don't mean it!

Sam Walton, the founder of Wal-Mart, once said, 'Nothing else can substitute for a few well chosen, well timed, sincere words of praise. They're absolutely free and worth a fortune.'

Confirming feedback is worth a fortune to you in terms of motivating your team and achieving your outcomes. It needs to be done well and we're going to look at how to do that. However, for the moment, let's look at the other side of the coin.

PRODUCTIVE FEEDBACK

This is about giving feedback on behaviour you're not happy with. As you spend time with your team you are going to see and hear things that are not going to ensure your *outcomes*. I'm emphasising the word 'outcomes' because at the end of the day these are what count. This is where you have to keep thinking and not reacting. It's inevitable that you'll see and hear things in your team that you don't like and you react to. If you do, engage your thinking mind and ask yourself, 'Is this something that is going to stop me achieving my outcome of a happy and motivated team who achieve their targets?' I've often had to 'bite my tongue' when I've seen or heard something that would not be the way I'd do it.

As I've made the point before in this book, results or as I like to call them, outcomes, are what matter to the Motivational Manager. If you see or hear something that's going to stop you achieving your outcomes, then you need to do something about it. If it's not going to affect your outcomes – keep your mouth shut!

Competencies: I'm not a fan

You may work in an organisation that has a competency program. These organisations have a list of behavioural competencies for a particular role and managers are required to rate team members on each one. They then 'encourage' the team member to work on the competencies they lack and the manager 'rates' the team member again at a later date.

This approach suits human resources departments as it imposes an ordered process on staff development. The only thing is – it doesn't work.

In an article in the *Gallup Management Journal*, Marcus Buckingham cites an experiment conducted in the late 1950s by the British and American military to develop the 'perfect' officer. The idea was to define the behaviours of the perfect officer, measure each person on these behaviours and then train each person to develop the behaviours he didn't naturally have.

Forty years later, after several attempts to tweak and redesign it, the military decided to abandon this approach to leadership development because it didn't work. It didn't measurably improve productivity, customer satisfaction, staff retention, attendance records or any other real-world measures of performance.

Ironically, many business organisations have now adopted the competency approach to developing people.

I once did some customer service training with a large organisation for their customer service agents. At the end of the training the human resources manager asked me to complete a competency document for each attendee. There were two computer-based forms to be completed with nearly a hundred statements. I was to tick the appropriate box, choosing from unsatisfactory to totally fantastic. I tried to explain to the HR manager that I didn't feel that I'd spent enough time with the participants to make a judgement; however, she insisted.

If you have this type of procedure in your organisation then you're just going to have to work with it. However, Motivational Managers rebel against it and I would encourage you to make your feelings known to your manager in a structured and positive way. I'll give you some ideas on how to do this later in the chapter.

As a manager, I'm not too concerned if a sales person doesn't fill in a report as per the company way if they're bringing in the orders and ensuring that the customers are happy. I would, however, evaluate the sales person's report writing in terms of how it affects my overall efficiency. If it affected my outcomes then I'd do something about it.

Competency programs are well-intentioned. However, they won't help you achieve your outcomes as a manager and they could demotivate your team.

> *Competency programs are well-intentioned. However, they won't help you achieve your outcomes as a manager.*

WHAT TO DO WHEN ONE OF THE TEAM ISN'T PERFORMING WELL

Let's look at what to do when one of your team isn't performing in a way that will achieve your outcomes. There are three things a manager could do.

1. Ignore them

Sadly, this is what happens too often when a manager sees or hears something he or she is not happy about. For example, a manager overhears one of her team speaking to a customer. The team member is using words and a tone of voice that are causing the customer to react badly. The manager thinks, 'That really isn't good enough. I'll let it go this time, but if I hear him speaking that way again to a customer I'll speak to him.' A few days later the manager overhears the team member speak to a customer in a similar way. The manager thinks, 'One more chance, but if I hear that again then I really will speak to him.' Eventually the manager comes down on the team member like a ton of bricks and all hell breaks loose.

Why does the manager do this? You'll know why you ignored behaviour you've been unhappy with; I've done it as a manager and I know why I did!

Time

Managers will often cite lack of time as a reason for not addressing poor behaviour. You don't need me to tell you about the pressures put on your time. However, as I said in Chapter 4, managers often don't see the value in spending time with their people. You need to find the time to deal with poor behaviour as soon as you observe it. Look at it this way: if you can nip it in the bud now, then you could save a great deal of time at a later date. Remember – 'Procrastination is the thief of time.'

> *You need to find the time to deal with poor behaviour as soon as you observe it.*

It's not that important

There is sometimes a case for ignoring poor behaviour. We might genuinely believe that it is a one-off and it probably won't happen again. You sometimes run the risk of being 'picky' and that can demotivate the team member. If someone turns up late and you know that they're always very prompt, then you may decide to ignore it. However, it is a judgement call and you really have to be honest with yourself. Are you ignoring it for the right reason or are you avoiding the confrontation?

Maybe it'll just go away

It's easy to tell ourselves that it probably won't happen again and dismiss it from our minds. Remember the Five Factors of

Success. Number five is Courage and that's what the Motivational Manager needs. These issues won't go away, if you deal with them as they happen, you'll make your life so much easier in the long run. You know it makes sense.

I don't want the hassle

We often perceive that if we speak to a team member about poor performance then they'll react badly. Well they might, and then again they might not. It all comes down to what I said earlier about your perception of whether you're comfortable giving or receiving feedback. It's not about how *you* feel it's how your team member feels about it. They might feel okay about having poor performance pointed out. Perhaps they won't. However, a lot of it comes down to how you speak to them. Keep reading and I'll show you how.

I don't want to demotivate them

This is so true and as I said earlier, there is sometimes a case for ignoring. However, you are also in danger of demotivating your team by not doing something about poor behaviour. Your people will know when they're not doing their best – and they know that you know. If you decide to ignore it then the team member feels you don't care and that's when they become demotivated.

I don't know what to do

Sometimes when a manager sees or hears poor behaviour they don't know how best to handle it. I made the point in Chapter 1 that many managers just aren't trained to deal with situations that arise with their team members; I know that I wasn't when I started as a manager. If we haven't been trained to do something then it's often much easier to ignore it and hope it goes away.

What happens if you ignore?

As you'll see from the above, there are several reasons for ignoring poor behaviour, and this is what happens if you do.

The team member continues to behave poorly

If you don't say anything then it's pretty obvious that the team member will continue with the poor behaviour and make no effort to improve. They're not necessarily doing whatever it is deliberately (although they might be and we'll come back to this), they may be doing it because they don't know any other way. It may be a lack of training or a misunderstanding of what's required.

They think you don't care

As I said above, your team members will often know when they're not doing well. If you don't do anything about it then they'll think that you're not interested and they have no incentive to improve. The majority of people don't like to be in this situation and it gives them a reason to look for another job.

The rest of the team notice

Don't think for one minute that you're the only person who notices the poor behaviour – the other team members do also. If you aren't seen to be doing something about poor behaviour then you'll lose credibility in the eyes of your team. Of course that doesn't mean you need to speak to the person who isn't performing in front of their colleagues. However, they'll know if you're taking action or not.

> *If you aren't seen to be doing something about poor behaviour then you'll lose credibility in the eyes of your team.*

The customer is affected

Another obvious one, but if there is a member of your team who is performing poorly then there's a good chance that the customer will suffer. And as a result your business will suffer and you won't achieve your outcomes.

You'll get stressed

As you know, this book is about achieving outcomes and avoiding stress. Ignoring poor behaviour will cause you to get stressed. You know you've ignored it, it preys on your mind and it'll probably give you more hassle at the end of the day.

> *Ignoring poor behaviour will cause you to get stressed.*

The team member leaves

They either leave for another job or you end up having to get rid of them. This gives you more hassle in terms of being short of staff and having to recruit and train new people.

So there are a lot of good reasons not to ignore poor behaviour. What are the other choices?

2. Shoot them

Only joking. However, some managers aren't too far off this. They come down hard on team members who aren't performing. They let them know right there and then how they feel and that the performance isn't good enough.

Let me ask you to think of a time when somebody reprimanded you. It might have been a teacher at school, a parent or a boss; how did you feel at the time? I do this exercise on some of my seminars and people come up with a whole range of feelings:

Annoyed – embarrassed – stupid – angry – victimised – unfairly treated – resentful – low self-esteem – lack of respect – dislike of the person doing the reprimand.

So what happens if you reprimand?

Some of the above

I'm sure you can remember experiencing some of the above feelings when you were reprimanded. I know I certainly did. Do you want your people to feel that way? Is it conducive to a happy and motivated team and is it going to help you achieve your outcomes? Somehow, I don't think so.

The team member gets stressed

All of the above feelings can lead to stress. And what will stress lead to? More days off work, poor service to customers, more hassle for you.

I have seen so many managers who come down hard on their people and then wonder why their team members always seem to have so many colds and flu and so many days off work. And of course, some of these people are spending their 'sick days' being interviewed for new jobs.

You get stressed

As a Motivational Manager, that is what you are trying to avoid. Having to reprimand someone is stressful for you; if they also take days of work then that adds to your stress.

They might just comply

If you reprimand one of your team for behaviour you're unhappy about then they're likely to respond by complying and improve temporarily. I'm sure you've seen the situation where the person being reprimanded says, 'Sorry about that boss, I won't do it again.' They comply for a short while and then they do it again. Many people being reprimanded see it as the boss 'having a go' and believe that it will all blow over.

They become demotivated

If you reprimand someone then it's very likely that they'll totally switch off. They then just go through the motions and do just enough to get by. This is sometimes known as 'Quit and stay' or as 'RIP' (resign in place).

I told the story in Chapter 1 about my time as a salesman for a welding company. My supervisor there was continually telling me what I was doing wrong. I was reprimanded for not doing enough demonstrations, not getting enough orders and having dust on the dashboard of my car. I became totally demoralised and found it even harder to get orders. Naturally, I spent a lot of my time looking for a new job. The day I resigned my supervisor's boss told me what a great guy I was and how I was showing so much promise. Of course it was too late by then.

They spread discontent

A team member who has been reprimanded is likely to spread discontent in your team. They'll tell the rest of the guys their side of the story and naturally they'll bad-mouth you. It's then possible that team morale will drop. The team think it's a shame that their poor colleague has been 'picked on' and that you'll probably pick on them next.

They give poor service

Just imagine a situation where you've just reprimanded one of your team and the next person they speak to is a customer. It doesn't take a genius to work out that the customer might receive less than excellent service. The team member doesn't necessarily set out to give the customer bad service, but their approach and tone of voice with the customer is hardly going to be enthusiastic.

A seminar participant once told me that she had been reprimanded by her manager for not smiling enough at customers.

She worked in a retail department store and her manager had been watching her on one of the security cameras. Can you imagine the sort of smiles given to the customer after that reprimand? I don't think they'd be too genuine.

You have to do more interviewing

If you take the reprimand route to deal with poor behaviour then you could spend a great deal of your time interviewing for new people. Some people take reprimands as part of their job. Many more are unwilling to accept them, particularly in areas

> *Those who accept reprimands as part of the job are unlikely to be happy, motivated and productive workers.*

where there are other jobs to be had. However, those who accept reprimands as part of the job are unlikely to be happy, motivated and productive workers.

They never do it again

One result of a reprimand is that the team member may not repeat the poor behaviour again. I can remember reprimands that I've had for poor behaviour – not that I had too many of them. I vowed to myself that I would never do it again. However, I can also remember thinking, 'And I'm not going to work for someone who treats me like that.'

You don't want your team members to repeat poor behaviour but you also don't want any of the other horrors described above. However, there is something you can do to deal effectively with poor behaviour and that's coaching.

3. Coach them

Coaching is about finding out the cause of poor performance or behaviour and discussing with the team member about how to put it right. The team member might respond immediately to coaching and improve the situation. However, the improvement may not always be permanent and you may have to do further coaching.

> *Coaching is about finding out the cause of poor performance or behaviour and discussing with the team member about how to put it right.*

When I suggest coaching to some managers, they see it as some kind of touchy-feely, softly-softly approach. Let me assure you right now – it's not! It's about telling the team member what you're not happy with, listening to what they have to say and agreeing a way forward.

The goal is to achieve a change in behaviour that the team member is committed to and helps you achieve your outcomes. So let's look at the benefits of coaching.

The team member feels good

I asked you earlier to think of a time when you were repri-manded and how you felt. Now think of a time when somebody – a teacher, parent, boss – coached, taught or encouraged you to get better at something. When I ask this question at seminars I get responses such as, 'I felt good – inspired – motivated – pleased – confident – wanted to do better.' This is what you're aiming for in your team.

More productive behaviour

The first objective of coaching is to resolve the poor behaviour. If it's done properly then that's what you'll achieve. However, there are other benefits.

The team member knows what's expected

Coaching allows you to make it very clear to your team members what is expected of them. Many managers fall into the trap of assuming that the team member knows what is expected. This is the reason for many examples of poor behaviour, such as:

- The team member didn't know reports had to be submitted by the 15th of the month.

- They didn't know they could give the customer their money back.

- They didn't know they had to be on time for the meeting.

I mentioned in Chapter 2 about, 'seeing it how they see it'. You might believe that you should always be dead on time for a meeting, but your team member may think that five or ten minutes either way makes no difference. Coaching allows you to calmly make clear what's expected.

The team member is motivated to change

As we've discussed before, the only real motivation is internal motivation. Coaching allows you to create the environment in which team members make the decision to change for themselves. This means that they're more committed to the change and it's more likely to happen. It's also easier on you because you don't have to 'drive' the team members to make the changes.

They know you care

If you coach in the way we're coming on to look at, your people will see you as supportive and understanding. They'll know that you're not just picking on them and they'll understand that you're looking for a win-win situation.

It ensures a happy and motivated team

That means better results, you achieving your outcomes and much less stress all round.

Fewer warning interviews

If you coach poor behaviour as and when it occurs then you're likely to have far fewer warning interviews. As we discussed earlier, the manager who ignores poor behaviour lets the situation build up and then finds himself in the 'warning' situation.

Coaching v reprimand

Let me give some further thoughts on what I mean by coaching. Imagine for a moment that you are coaching an athlete who's going for Olympic Gold. A reprimand would be, 'That was a totally useless performance, you're never going to make the Olympics with a time like that and you'd better shape up your ideas.'

Alternatively, you could say, 'That was a good performance, I liked the way you came out of the blocks. All we need to do is find a way to shave another two seconds off your time and you're going to win an Olympic Gold Medal. I've got some ideas on how we can do that. What do you think we can do?'

Which style is going to get the results you require? I know which one I've found to work.

THE WAY TO COACH

Whether it's Confirming or Productive feedback, it needs to be done in a particular way and the same rules apply for both.

Confirming feedback

Have you ever heard yourself say to a team member, 'You're really great' – 'You're a star' – 'I think you're brilliant' – 'You're doing a great job?'

It's got to be a plus point that you're giving Confirming feedback and there's nothing intrinsically wrong with any of the statements above; however, they could be better. There is a danger that these statements could come across as a bit patronising. Managers who find it a bit difficult to give Confirming feedback might also feel uncomfortable with these types of statements.

One of the other reasons for giving Confirming feedback is to get more of the same behaviour; the statements above may not guarantee that. Let me give you an example of what I mean.

Fred has just submitted a report that you're pleased with and you decide to tell him so: 'That's a great report Fred; you're brilliant at writing reports!' But what made the report great and why is Fred so brilliant at writing them?

It would have been better to say, 'I liked the way you structured that report Fred. The words you used and the use of diagrams made it easy for me to understand. Thank you for the time you have obviously put into it.' Fred now knows what it is you like about his report and is more likely to write in a similar way in the future.

This is what we call being **Descriptive**. You are describing to the team member what you saw or heard that you liked. This carries much more weight than a 'Well done!' Managers who are uncomfortable with Confirming feedback find this easier to do because it takes the 'emotion' out of the statement. There is also less risk of sounding patronising.

Productive feedback

It's even more important to use descriptive statements when you see or hear something you're not happy with.

We talked at great length in Chapter 2 about thinking instead of reacting; this is where you need to do a lot of thinking.

It's so easy to react when a team member does or says something we don't like. We say things like, 'You've got the wrong attitude!'–

'You're hopeless!' – 'That was a stupid way to deal with that situation!' – 'You'll need to shape up!' – 'You're not very responsible!' Statements like these will only get the team member's back up and won't get the change in behaviour you want.

Let's say that one of your team turns up late for the third time in a week. You decided to ignore the first two late situations but this third time has made you angry. You might say, 'You've got the wrong attitude to this job, you're always late and I'm not having it. If you're late again you'll receive an official warning.'

That statement is not descriptive, it's reactive. It stresses you, it demotivates the team member and it's unlikely to resolve the situation. A descriptive statement would be, 'I'm unhappy with the fact that you've been late for work three times this week. I'm willing to hear your reasons for being late and agree with you how we can prevent this happening in the future.' You're letting the team member know that you're not prepared to accept their lateness but you're willing to hear their side of the story.

When you describe performance, you are focusing on specific behaviour. You describe what you see and what you hear in clear terms that the team member can also see, hear and understand.

I've been in a situation like this where a team member is turning up late. After some discussion it turns out that there's some domestic problem, with children or some other family situation that's causing them to be late. Of course, you also get the person who's just cutting it too fine in timing their journey to work.

We've looked at the fact that members of your team see the world in a different way from you and from each other. Some people are very particular about being on time and others take a much more relaxed view. They think it's okay to arrive for work ten or fifteen minutes late because they often work through their lunch hour or stay late in the evening. If you're not prepared to accept that then you need to tell them so. However, you may wish to make a judgement call and accept their timekeeping. At the end of the day it comes back to outcomes – are they producing the results? You may have to consider how their timekeeping affects the other members of the team.

> *Using descriptive statements and coaching the individual will resolve the situation in terms of your interests and those of the team members.*

I've only talked about lateness. However, there are many other situations where you will be required to give some Productive feedback and coach people. It could be the way the team member speaks to a customer or a colleague. It could be for failing to produce the required results. Whatever it is, using descriptive statements and coaching the individual will resolve the situation in terms of your interests and those of the team members.

Let's look at the detail of giving feedback. Whether you want to reinforce behaviour (Confirming feedback) or change unacceptable behaviour (Productive feedback), there are certain steps you need to follow to make it work.

HOW TO MAKE FEEDBACK EFFECTIVE

1. Do it ASAP

When you see or hear something you do or don't like you need to say something right away. If it's Confirming feedback it's not much use saying something months later: 'I liked the way you handled that difficult customer a couple of months ago Dave.' Dave is going to have a bit of a problem remembering that situation and the effect of the feedback is totally wasted.

It also makes sense to give Dave Productive feedback as soon as you see or hear something you don't like. If you don't do it right away then Dave will assume that you didn't notice or that it doesn't matter or that you don't care. Again, it's totally useless to bring up something you're not happy about months later. It's back to what we said earlier about ignoring the situation. If you say, 'Dave, I didn't like what you said to that angry customer a few weeks ago', don't be surprised if Dave hasn't a clue what you're talking about.

2. Do it in private

This seems like the most obvious thing to say but I still observe managers giving a member of their team some Productive feedback in front of other people, be they colleagues or customers. Of course, it's usually more of a reprimand.

I think that some managers believe that if they're seen and heard giving some feedback then it will have an effect on the other team members. You bet it will – it will totally demotivate them!

Some managers also believe that if it's Confirming feedback, the good news, then it's motivational to do it in front of colleagues. It could motivate the other people in the team to hear one of their colleagues receive some good news but it might also embarrass the person on the receiving end and have a negative effect.

So do it in private whenever you can.

However, this can often be difficult in today's open-plan offices.

You obviously have the choice of finding a meeting room or an empty office somewhere. It would be best to do this if you were giving Productive feedback, the not-so-good news, as this is bound to take longer and be more involved that Confirming feedback.

If you were giving one of your team some Confirming feedback in an open-plan office, then it would be okay to pull up a chair and quietly say, 'I liked the way you empathised with that customer Mary' or 'That report you produced on our maintenance schedule was well written and easy to understand Frank.' The people round about don't have to hear this and if you pick your moment well, they could be on the phone or busy with their own job.

If it's really difficult to get some privacy then you could always send a note. E-mail if you wish but just think how motivating a hand-written note could be, complimenting one of your team on a job well done.

3. Check that it's okay to speak

I mentioned this in Chapter 4 when I said, 'Don't sneak up on your people.' Always check that it's okay to speak. If one of your team has just finished speaking to a customer on the phone, they might have some admin things to do before they forget. If you interrupt then you risk being responsible for a customer not getting something they were promised. It's only good manners to check before speaking and your people will respect you for it.

4. Announce your intentions

If your people are not used to receiving regular feedback, what do you think runs through their mind when you pull up a chair or ring them on the phone? Your right – they think it's bad news, that they've done something wrong or there's a problem.

It's important to tell them up front what you want to speak about. You might say, 'Jill, I've just read your last report and I'd like to give you some good news.' You then go on to give them some Confirming feedback and remember to make it descriptive.

If it was some aspect of their behaviour that you weren't happy about and you were about to give some Productive feedback, then you might say, 'Joe, I couldn't help overhearing your last telephone call to a customer. It's something I'm concerned about but it's not a big thing. On a scale of one to ten this would probably be a three.' You would then go on to give Joe some Productive feedback.

Once your team members become used to receiving regular feedback, they will be much more open and responsive. They'll know that you're always the first person to tell them when they've done something well and what you like about their behaviour. They'll also know that you'll always tell them when you're unhappy with something they've done.

> *Once your team members become used to receiving regular feedback, they will be much more open and responsive.*

5. Tell them how *you* feel about their behaviour

Your people work for the same organisation as you but it's you they have to please. So make sure when you give feedback that it comes from you. That means not saying things like, 'The Company doesn't like their employees to speak to customers like that,' or, 'It's not up to me but you'd better improve your performance or you'll be in trouble.'

You need to use lots of 'I' messages. Get personally involved; say things like, 'I liked the way you told that customer that you'd deal with their problem yourself', or, 'I'm unhappy with the way you told that customer that it wasn't your responsibility', or, 'I believe there's another way to do that job.'

It's important to avoid 'You' messages such as, 'You're doing a great job.' This can come across as patronising and it isn't descriptive. Neither should you say, 'You shouldn't have done it that way.'

Using the 'You' word in Productive feedback could sound accusing and will possibly put your team member on the defensive. It then makes the job of giving feedback harder for you.

It's also not a good idea to say things like, 'It's come to my attention,' or, 'Other people feel that you are not pulling your weight.' If you're the one giving the Productive feedback then you need to use 'I' messages.

6. Focus on one thing at a time

Don't confuse your team member with a whole list of behaviours. If it's Confirming feedback then you don't want to be saying, 'I like the way you handle customers and your reports are always done on time and it's great that you're achieving your target.' You're only diluting the whole feedback and it loses its impact.

If you are giving Productive feedback then you don't want to confuse your team member with a whole catalogue of behaviours that you're unhappy about. Sadly this seems to be the case with managers who don't give feedback on poor behaviour immediately. They allow things to go on and on and then they eventually explode. It's much better to deal with behaviour as and when it happens.

7. Be specific

When you are giving one of your team some feedback and coaching them, it's important to focus on job-related behaviour and not on the personality of the individual.

I mentioned in Chapter 4 that some managers don't feel comfortable giving feedback, either the good or the not so good. That's often because they subconsciously see it as a comment on the person's character rather than the behaviour. If you feel a bit uncomfortable giving feedback, try to focus on the person's behaviour on the job in terms of how they conducted a particular task. That's what you're giving feedback on, not them as a person. It becomes easier if you use 'I' messages and are very descriptive about what you've seen or heard. You could say something like, 'I liked the way you tidied up the workshop after you finished that job – thank you Fred.' You're trying to get the balance between being human but also businesslike.

8. Include the customer and the organisation

Whenever appropriate, relate what your feedback is about to how the customer was affected. This of course could be an internal or an external customer. You could also relate it to how the organisation was affected, if relevant.

9. Get input

When giving Productive feedback, it's important to get the team member's input. You might say, 'I'm unhappy that this is the third time this month that your report has been late Joanne. However, I'm willing to listen to what you have to say and discuss how we can resolve this situation.'

You need to listen to what Joanne has to say, then discuss and agree what's going to happen in the future. You then need to set a date when you'll check back with Joanne as to the progress she's made.

It's important that the team member understands that this isn't just a whinge from you or that you'll probably forget about it by tomorrow. This is something that needs to be resolved and it won't go away.

You could say something like, 'Okay Joanne, you've agreed that you're going to get your reports in on time from now on; let's check back this time next week and see how it's going.' You then need to put it in your diary and check back when you said you would.

It's also important to check the team member understands what's required and that they make a commitment to change. Let the feedback sink in and give them every opportunity to have their say.

Perhaps they might not be capable of making the changes that they're agreeing to. Remember what we said in Chapter 2 about not making people what they're not. They may not have the skills and knowledge and you need to identify that.

There is no point in Joanne telling you that she'll get her reports in on time if she doesn't have a clue how to do that. This is where you need to do some coaching or take another course of action.

In Chapter 8 we'll concentrate on solving problems that arise with your team members.

10. Don't leave them low

This is particularly important after giving Productive feedback. As I said earlier, this isn't an attack on the person; it's about job-related behaviour. A team member should come out of a Productive feedback session with their sense of self-worth intact.

After you've coached them and agreed what action they're going to take, you might want to say, 'Okay Joanne, thank you for your time, I'm going to get myself a cup of coffee, can I get you one?', or, 'I hope you enjoy your trip to the theatre tonight, it sounds like a great show.'

You're getting the message across that 'I'm not angry with you. I have nothing against you personally. I just need you to behave in a manner that meets the necessities of the job.' (Of course, you're not using these words!)

Forget the sandwich technique

Many managers have been told to use the 'sandwich technique' when giving Productive feedback and coaching their people. Let me give you an example: 'Fred, I'm really pleased with how you've been progressing since you joined us and you're doing a great job. However, you're not dealing with enough customers and we're missing our call targets. I'd like you to tighten up on this. Anyway, thanks for all you've done so far and keep up the good work.'

Have you ever said something along these lines? You probably needed Fred to increase the number of calls he made but you didn't want to upset or demoralise him. The only problem is that Fred may not get the message. The importance of it may be seriously diluted. He may hear it as, 'Fred, you're doing a brilliant job, you just need to do a few more calls but it's not that important.' What happens then is that Fred continues to fail with his number of calls.

The 'sandwich' technique doesn't work. It lets you off the hook and it's mealy mouthed. Be direct with your people and they'll respect you

> *Be direct with your people and they'll respect you more for it.*

more for it. You're also much more likely to get the change in behaviour you require.

If you're unhappy with some aspect of a team member's performance then you need to tell them so and coach them if required. The skill is in doing it in a way that is effective and doesn't lower the morale of the individual. If you follow the ten points listed above then you're much more likely to get the changes you need without lowering morale and without raising your level of stress.

Up as well as down

So far we've been looking at feedback and coaching for your team members. The reason we're doing this is:

1 To reinforce behaviour and motivate your people (Confirming feedback);

2 To change behaviour that will stop you achieving your outcomes (Productive feedback).

Your goal is to give feedback that motivates or at least doesn't demotivate your team. You also want to minimise your levels of stress.

> *Your goal is to give feedback that motivates or at least doesn't demotivate your team.*

However, there are other people who will affect your ability to achieve your outcomes and may have a negative effect on your levels of stress – your colleagues and your boss (particularly your boss).

As well as dealing with your team every day you also have to deal with people in other departments, often senior to you. I'm also pretty sure that your boss figures pretty much in your life. These people also need feedback, both Confirming and Productive.

Next time you're dealing with a colleague in another department and they give you some good service, use the feedback rules above. Say something like, 'I liked the way you sent that information within the time you promised – thank you for that Mary.' I think you'll find that it improves your chances of receiving similar service in the future.

And don't be afraid to give your colleagues some Productive feedback if they're not behaving as you'd like them to; again, use the rules above. I'm always hearing managers complain that their boss behaves in a way that gives them problems, stops them achieving outcomes and stresses them out. However, these managers fail to communicate their concerns to their boss.

There's still a culture in many organisations that doesn't allow the boss to be challenged. It's a case of the boss tells me what to do and it's my job to do what I'm told. It's also the case that managers don't want to say anything to their boss for fear of being perceived as negative or a whinger.

Why not try giving your boss some Confirming feedback? The occasional compliment or descriptive thank you will work wonders on your relationship. And if the boss is doing or saying something you're not happy with, give her some Productive feedback using the rules above. If you follow these rules, then you're much less likely to be seen as a whinger.

6
Be a Believer

GET SOMEONE ELSE TO DO YOUR WORK

They say that the further up the management tree you go in any organisation, the fewer bits of paper you'll find on a manager's desk. The guys at the bottom of the tree are buried in the stuff and the manager has a nice clear desk.

I can remember it being like that for me in a company where I was a middle manager. My job title was Sales Operations Manager and I was responsible for things like promotional activity, telesales, sales targets, budgets and all the admin functions. My boss, Tom, was the Sales Director.

I remember one report I produced for Tom. He asked me to come up with some recommendations for a new sales procedure that he wanted to implement. I spent hours on that report, doing the research, making phone calls and having meetings with colleagues. Eventually I had the masterpiece typed up with all my recommendations on what action we should take; even if I do say so myself, it was an excellent report. I took it into Tom's office and he read it through; he asked a few questions and queried some of the detail. Eventually he said, 'Well done, excellent, I suggest you go ahead and implement this.' He went to hand me back my report and I said, 'You keep that Tom, that's your copy.' He grunted something, took the report, screwed it up and threw it in the bin. My immediate inclination was to launch myself across his desk and rip out his windpipe. Luckily I resisted the temptation but boy did I feel angry!

It was only later, after I'd cooled down, that I thought about the matter with a bit more logic and less emotion. What did I expect him to do with this piece of paper? Fondle it longingly and admire it on his desk? I don't think so. He'd read the report, he'd come to a decision and decided to move on. Tom knew that the report would be filed on my computer and that there'd be a hard copy stuffed into the bulging filing cabinet beside my desk.

I learned several lessons that day;

1   Don't keep so much paper hanging about.

2   Make decisions quickly and move on.

3   Get someone else to do your work!

I'm being flippant about that third part. However, as a manager you need to ensure that you're not doing any tasks that you don't really need to. There's a saying that many managers should pay some attention to – 'Only do it if only you can do it.'

So – don't do it

We're now getting into the area of Empowerment which was first introduced in the 1980s and became a bit of a management buzz word. However, I believe that it's one of the most promising but least understood concepts in management today.

As you'll have gathered by reading this book so far, I'm a fairly down-to-earth, practical sort of person. I'm not big into management theories unless I can see the benefits for me; I see a great deal of benefit for managers and team leaders in Empowerment.

I was empowered by my boss Tom although I don't think he used it as a management tool or even understood what it was all about. However, his way of managing me by empowerment had benefits for both of us.

The benefits of Empowerment

Benefits for Tom

I described my job above. However, many of the tasks that I carried out would, in some organisations, be Tom's responsibility. These were tasks that I could do much better than him. This meant that part of his job was being done better than he could have done it and ultimately made him look good.

With me doing many of the things that would normally be tasks for him, left him clear to do other things. One of Tom's main tasks and one he was particularly good at was negotiating contracts with customers. And I must say, something he could do much better than me.

Our products were beer and other drinks. However, it wasn't just a matter of negotiating a price with the customer. Our company lent money to the customer on the understanding that he sold our products alone. This was standard practice in the UK beer industry and there were various types of loans that could be negotiated with the customer. As I said, Tom was particularly good at this and spent a great deal of his time on it. As a result, he pulled in a great deal of business.

Now you might be thinking, 'It's all right for Tom but what about poor old Alan?'

Benefits for Alan

I was very happy with the situation. I had more responsibility than I might normally have. I was able to do my own thing and run things more or less how I wanted; all I had to do was regularly check things with Tom.

So at the end of the day, he was happy, I was happy and the business was happy. Tom was achieving his outcomes and he wasn't getting stressed. I was achieving my outcomes, I was learning, developing and I was enjoying my job.

WHY USE EMPOWERMENT?

As you're very much aware, this book is about motivating your team and minimising your stress; that's why I'm encouraging *you* to empower your team. However, I'm aware that some organisations are into Empowerment and some aren't. Some talk about it a lot and tell you that they practise Empowerment. However, in my experience it doesn't happen nearly as much as it should. It may not happen in your organisation but that doesn't mean that it can't happen in your team. You can create a culture of Empowerment in your team which will have benefits for you and your people.

> *You can create a culture of Empowerment in your team which will have benefits for you and your people.*

Let's just reflect for a moment on what *does* motivate people at work. There has been all sorts of research done over the years and many books have been written about it (believe me, I've read most of them). I'm going to pull all of this information together in the last chapter of the book but for the moment, let's consider some of the factors and not in any specific order.

We've already looked at feedback and acknowledgement. The majority of people will be motivated at work if they believe that their manager cares about them and gives them feedback, recognition and praise for a job well done. And just in case you've forgotten, we call this Confirming feedback.

However, people are motivated by other factors, such as the work itself. You might call this job satisfaction. Your team will be motivated if they:

- Find the work interesting.

- Know what's expected of them.

- Have the opportunity to do what they do best.

- Are encouraged to develop, learn and grow.

- Have the feeling of being in on things, ownership and involvement.

These motivational needs can be satisfied by empowering your people, so let's take a closer look at what Empowerment is all about.

UNLEASH THE POWER

Empowerment is about utilising the knowledge, skill, experience and motivational power that's already within your people.

> *Empowerment is about utilising the knowledge, skill, experience and motivational power that's already within your people.*

The majority of people in teams and organisations are severely underutilised. Your team have probably much more to offer in terms of skill, knowledge and experience, and if you utilise that you will achieve your outcomes and you'll motivate them.

If you're not sure about this then think about yourself for a moment. Do you think your manager uses your skill, knowledge and experience? Do you feel involved? Do you have a sense of ownership? Are your opinions considered? Do you have the opportunity to develop and grow? If you have answered 'yes' to these questions then you're in an unusual situation and very fortunate. The majority of managers that I work with complain that they don't experience any of these factors.

I've proved to myself with the teams that I managed that Empowerment works. However, initially it's easier said than done. There needs to be quite a shift in thinking and a change of habits. Remember, the majority of people in work today are brought up with programs that say, 'This is my job, I do what I'm told to do, I'm not paid to think and I'm not taking responsibility.'

So for you as the manager, it's not just a case of telling your team that they're empowered and that they have the authority to make decisions. They'll probably just see it as you offloading some of your work onto them and they won't respond positively to that.

LET PEOPLE KNOW WHAT'S HAPPENING

If you want an empowered team then they need to know what's happening in the organisation and what's happening in the team. If they don't know what's going on then they can't be expected to make good decisions.

> *If you want an empowered team then they need to know what's happening in the organisation and what's happening in the team.*

Most organisations nowadays supply information about what's happening in the business and encourage managers to brief their teams. If there's no procedure to brief you on what's happening in your organisation, then let your manager know that you need that information so that you can brief your team. Use the procedure for Productive feedback that we discussed in the last chapter.

Give your team all the information you can, such as:

- How the organisation makes money

- What the costs are in running the company

- How it makes a profit

- Sales figures

- How to read a balance sheet

- How to read a profit and loss statement

- Customer complaints

- Customer compliments

- Absenteeism

- Surveys and research

- Marketing plans

- New products

- New policies and procedures

- Anything that relates directly to your team

- Anything that affects the business or the organisation

If you don't feel confident delivering any of this information, then seek help from your colleagues. If, for example, finance is not 'your thing', then get one of your colleagues from the finance department to brief the team.

I was working with some managers at one of my clients recently and they were complaining that their senior manager never came out of his office to speak to their teams. My answer to that was, 'Ask him!' Some of the managers were giving me 'I shouldn't have to ask him' comments and obviously weren't going to do what I suggested. However, Bill, one of the managers, spoke to me a week later: 'I asked the boss to speak to my team and he did. It was a big success and they really appreciated getting information from a senior manager.'

As I said in Chapter 2, we need to think about the programs we all live our lives by and question whether they're holding us back or not. I now know that Bill will do what it takes to ensure that his team knows what's going on in the organisation.

I recently attended a seminar on environmental issues in industry (not usually my subject but it was a good opportunity for networking). The presenter outlined a case history company where the employees were briefed on waste management within their organisation. Over a period of months the people in the business started to take actions of their own volition to reduce waste. They were concerned about the amount of money that the business was losing in handling waste and realised it could be money in their pocket.

They want to be involved

Your team want to know, they want to feel 'in on things' and be involved. They want to know the goals of the organisation, the goals of the team and what their role is in achieving these goals.

> *Your team want to know, they want to feel 'in on things' and be involved.*

Some years ago when I was working at the brewery, I was invited along one day to a regional manager's sales meeting. This was his weekly meeting with his team and he told me that he'd also invited a couple of the delivery guys to sit in. I was initially quite surprised at this because like many of my colleagues I didn't have a particularly high regard for these delivery guys. These were the people who drove the trucks and unloaded kegs of beer and crates into pubs and hotels. They always seemed a belligerent group to me, always complaining about something and generally being unhelpful. I'd been involved in several situations where I had to solve an unhappy customer situation caused by a delivery driver. Of course, looking back on it now, it was just another case of people who were poorly managed. And of course, at that time, my thinking was pretty narrow as well.

There were three delivery guys at the sales meeting sitting round the table with the rest of the sales team. Initially they were fairly quiet but once the meeting really got going they became more involved. They wanted to know why the sales team weren't finding more new business, why certain accounts had been lost, why we were selling the products we were and why we didn't introduce new ones. They made some excellent suggestions and provided information to the sales team that they'd never heard before.

Ironically, these delivery people spent more time face to face with our customers than anyone else in the company did. They were delivering to customers every week and sometimes twice a week. And they had good relationships with many of these customers.

This meeting certainly opened my eyes to the fact that people want to know and they want to be involved in the business. If you let them, then it can be hugely beneficial.

LEAVE THEM ALONE

I've seen the situation happen many times when I've been running seminars for managers. Every time we have a break (and on my seminars we have many) certain managers are immediately on their mobile phones. They're checking with their teams; I can hear them saying, 'What's happening, any problems, what are the figures like, has the boss been round?' I've seen managers spend the whole of the coffee break on the phone and be reluctant to come back into the seminar.

These managers just can't leave their team alone; they need to be checking all the time. You need to be able to leave your team for a day, a week or the two weeks when

> *You need to be able to leave your team for a day, a week or the two weeks when you're on holiday and know that things will run smoothly.*

you're on holiday and know that things will run smoothly.

I know what I said in Chapters 4 and 5 about spending time with your people and you need to do this. However, if you're away from your team for a day then a phone call at the end of the day will suffice. And if you can't manage that, what's the big deal?

When you do make that phone call, your goal should be to deliver some Confirming feedback rather than 'check up'. For example, if you are phoning your second in command or any of your team members you should be saying something like, 'Sounds like you've handled the situations of today really well, thanks Jane for being so responsible.'

> *Problems are solved on the spot, as soon as they arise. No front-line employee has to wait for a supervisor's permission.*

Jan Carlzon (1941–, Swedish business executive, CEO of SAS)

DECIDE THE BOUNDARIES

You do, however, need to make it clear to your team what the boundaries are; they need to be clear as to what they're empowered to do. This is not a case of 'You can do this and you can't do that.' It's more a case of 'This is as far as you can go.' If you're continually giving your team information about the organisation as we described above, then the boundaries will make sense.

Imagine you're running a sales team and they're always under pressure from customers to reduce prices. Naturally you want your team to sell at the highest possible price, so ensuring your profit targets are met. You know and your team know what your sales target is and how you're performing to target at any one time. They should also know what your profitability target is and what it costs to run the sales team. However, you still need to set boundaries. It is feasible to allow sales people a level of discount they can negotiate up to, obtain the customer's business and still ensure your profit targets are met. If, for example, every sale was discounted by 20 per cent and that still allowed you to make your profit target, then that could be the boundary. Every sales person would then know that they could offer the customer up to 20 per cent to obtain the business.

Many sales managers get nervous about this as they believe that their sales people will offer the customer 20 per cent discount as soon as they come under pressure. You have to trust your team; if you're giving them regular information and communicating your desire to increase your profits, then your team won't give away any more discount than they have to.

When you spend time with your team and you have one member who is giving too much discount too often, then you would give him some Productive feedback and coach him to do better. It follows that the sales people who give away very little discount receive some Confirming feedback. This will encourage them to continue along this path.

> *Your team need to know how far they can go to satisfy the customer.*

In a customer service job, your team need to know how far they can go to satisfy the customer; they need to be able to do what you do.

In too many organisations there is still the situation where a customer service person has to refer to the manager to solve the problem. The customer says, 'I'm not satisfied with your answer, I want to speak to a manager.' The manager then speaks to the customer and makes some form of concession. The results of this are:

1. It's another job for the manager to do that she really shouldn't be doing.

2. It demotivates the team member because they feel stupid and embarrassed in front of the customer.

I have a friend, Gill, who used to work in the returns department of a high street department store. This store was well known for its excellent returns policy. However, many customers took advantage of it. They would buy an item of clothing, wear it several times and then return it claiming it was the wrong fit or some other excuse. Gill was instructed to politely question the customer, and to point out if the garment was soiled or looked like it had been worn. She would then discourage the customer from obtaining a refund. However, if the customer insisted, Gill would have to summon her supervisor who would immediately refund the customer. Gill found this extremely annoying as she was often made to feel small in front of a customer who had no right to a refund. And of course, the supervisor's time could have been put to much better use if Gill had been empowered to make a decision which was ultimately best for the business.

Your team members need to be able to do for the customer what you can do for the customer. The dictionary defines Empowerment as 'to give power to' and this is what you need to do for your team. If you constantly communicate with them they will know what your outcomes are and how their decisions will affect those outcomes.

> *Your team members need to be able to do for the customer what you can do for the customer.*

This can be hard for many managers because they've been brought up to understand that managers make more important decisions than their team members; that they have more authority and power.

It's exactly the same between you and your manager; you should know what you're empowered to do. You shouldn't be running to your manager asking, 'Can I do this with my team? Can I do that with this customer?'

Whether your manager empowers you or not, this book is about *you*, how you get the best out of your team and how you minimise your stress. You can do that if you empower them.

ACCOUNTABLE AND RESPONSIBLE

Of course, if you empower your team members to make decisions, then they need to know that they're accountable and responsible for the results of their behaviour. That can be good and not so good. If it's good then it's an opportunity to deliver some Confirming feedback, a compliment and praise for a job well done.

Obviously it wouldn't work if they took all the credit for the good decisions they made and blamed you for all the not-so-good ones. However, it's all about how you handle the times when a not-so-good decision has been made.

If a manager comes down hard on a team member when a poor decision has been made, then you can wave goodbye to an empowered team. When a poor decision by a team member results in some kind of problem then it's important to find out what went wrong, how it can be fixed and what you and the team member can learn from it. And it's not a case of you as the manager fixing it; you need to agree a course of action with the team member that they're committed to.

Always remember that people learn and develop from mistakes, so don't always regard these as a big negative.

By minimising the fear of reprisal you're more likely to have a happy and motivated team who continue to be empowered. They're then more likely to make decisions that improve the quality of your outcomes and increase sales and profits.

Take risks

Picture the scene: your eleven-year-old son or daughter decides one Sunday morning that they're going to make breakfast and bring it to you in bed. Your first thoughts are: 'They'll make a mess of it, they'll break something or they might burn themselves.' So you say, 'Thank you for the offer, but it's best if I do it. You go and watch television and perhaps you can do it another time.' The result is that you demotivate the child and you send them a subconscious message that they're useless and you don't trust them. So you end up making your own breakfast and the child never learns how to do it.

With all these negative consequences, isn't it just worth the risk? Perhaps the kitchen will be a mess; maybe they will break something; and let's face it, what's the chance of them burning themselves? Surely it's worth the risk to motivate your child, give them a feeling of self-worth and send them the message that you believe in them.

It's exactly the same with your team; as they take on more responsibilities, they learn and develop. They also start to enjoy their work more and that in turn motivates them.

WHAT YOU EXPECT IS WHAT YOU GET

'You will never have an empowered team unless you believe in them and they know that you believe in them.' I made this point on a recent seminar and one manager said, 'I believe in my team and they know that.' So I asked him, 'How do they know? What is it that you do that let's them know that you believe in them?' 'I don't do anything,' he replied. 'They just know.' Now maybe his team members know and maybe they don't know that he believes in them – I suspect not. It's okay to know in your own head that you believe in your people. However, you need to be aware of how you communicate that feeling to them. You may be inadvertently sending the wrong message.

There's a concept in management know as the Pygmalion effect, sometimes known as the 'Self-fulfilling Prophecy'. It's based on a Greek legend about a sculptor named Pygmalion who created an ivory statue of his ideal woman. The result, which he named Galatea, was so beautiful that he fell in love with his own creation. He prayed to the Goddess Venus and his feeling for the statue was so strong that it brought her to life. The idea behind this legend is that an individual can affect how others behave through the power of their feelings about them.

I remember reading a story about some teenagers in an American high school class. As a cruel prank, the boys in the class decided that they would all ask out on a date the plainest and dullest girl in the class. The first two or three boys took turns to take the girl out on a date and pretended that they found her pretty and an interesting person to be with. The girl was a bit confused but only too pleased to have this attention lavished upon her. By the time it became the turn of some of the last boys to ask her out they were really looking forward to it. The plain and dull girl had responded to the attention being paid to her. She started to take more care of her appearance and developed a more confident outgoing demeanour. The result was she became a pretty and interesting person – she was affected by the power of the boys' feelings about her.

A study into the Pygmalion effect

Robert Rosenthal and Lenore Jacobson carried out a study in 1968 in which children aged six to twelve, all drawn from the same school, were given an IQ test. Before the next school year began, the teachers were given the names of those children who, on the basis of the test, were expected to be high achievers. In fact, Rosenthal and Jacobson had randomly picked these names from the class list. The test did not identify high achievers as the teachers had been led to believe. Any difference between these children and the rest of the class existed only in the heads of the teachers.

A second IQ test was conducted at the end of the year. Those children who had been identified as high achievers showed on average an increase of more than 12 points on their IQ scores. This compared to an increase of 8 points among the rest of the children.

The teachers also indicated that these 'special' children were better behaved, were more intellectually curious, had a greater chance of future success and were friendlier than their 'non-special' counterparts.

Of course, what had happened was that the teachers spent more time with the 'special' children, they were more enthusiastic about teaching them and unintentionally showed that they cared about them more than the other children.

Now you may be thinking that you're not a teacher and you're not dealing with children. However, your team members will respond in a very similar way, and how you feel about them is how they will turn out to be.

Are you sure you know them?

We all have a view about what our people are like. You have a view on what your team members are like. However, as we discussed earlier in the book, how well do you really know them?

A manager in one of my seminars was telling me about a fellow manager that she had regular dealings with. She told me that, up until recently, she didn't like him much and they didn't get on. However, they had recently attended a course together and she'd got to know her colleague manager much better. In the time they spent together she discovered another side to this person and now they get on much better.

Do you remember the quote by Abraham Lincoln that I mentioned earlier? Here it is again: 'I don't think I like that man; I must get to know him better.'

The way you treat your team members will be subtly influenced by what you expect from them.

I'd like you to think for a moment about how you might treat some new additions to your team. I'm going to describe these people to you and I would like you to think how you might treat them when they join you.

Susan is obese, she always seems to have something wrong with her and she does everything very slowly.

Adam has a view on everything, he's a real strong union guy and he's got some really left-wing views.

Mary always does as she's told and never gives any problems; she comes from an affluent family.

Just think about how you'll react to those people when they join your team. Bear in mind, of course, that I'm giving you my view of these people, not necessarily anyone else's.

You might be saying, 'I treat everyone the same until I get to know them.' However, remember what we said about our inbuilt programs in Chapter 2. What if you have a program that says, 'Fat people are lazy'? How might that affect how you treat Susan? We all have these inbuilt programs and they are all different; it is so easy to be influenced by them.

I was running a seminar at a client's office and I was discussing the arrangements for getting into the building and finding the training room with my client Dave. He explained to me that I'd have to make contact with the security guard at the reception desk. 'You'll not get much help from him,' says Dave. 'He's a typical security guard, a grumpy old so-and-so.'

My first response when I arrived at the office was to prepare for a battle with this 'typical' security guard. However, at the last moment I checked myself and decided to practise what I preach. I approached the security guard, told him who I was in a warm, friendly manner and asked for directions to the training room. John, as the name on his badge said he was, had to make a few phone calls to find out where my room was. In between these calls we exchanged some small talk and even managed some comments about the local football team's performance the night before. Initially, John was a bit grumpy but after a while he warmed up and ultimately couldn't have been more helpful. I was treating him with respect, I was getting to know him and expecting him to respond in a helpful manner – and that's how he responded.

Dave, of course, treated John like a 'typical' security guard who was grumpy and unhelpful – so that was how John responded.

Silent messages

It's not so much what you say to your team that communicates your expectations of them; it's more about how you behave. Your tone of voice, your facial expression and your body language will all communicate your expectations to your team members. Again, it's not so much what you say as how you say it.

You might say to one of your team, 'Joan, would you be willing to be responsible for the team's health and safety procedures?' If you say these words with a negative or quizzical look on your face and in a hesitant tone of voice, then don't be surprised if the answer is 'no'. Joan will sense from the look on your face and the tone of your voice if you believe she can do this job and take on the responsibility. You are much more likely to get a positive response if you look and sound like you expect a positive answer. It's your body language and tone that will tell Joan your expectations of her are high.

The caring manager often finds it difficult to create a culture of Empowerment because they always want to 'look after' the team member. It's similar to the loving mother who does everything for her son; she cooks, cleans up after him and irons his shirts. She has a program that tells her that because he's a male, he won't be able to do any of these things or he'll make a complete hash of them. As a result, the son never learns how to look after himself and grows up believing that he can't cook or iron a shirt. I'm sure there are many newly married wives who can attest to this.

If you believe that one of your team can't take care of an angry customer and you always have to step in then you're always going to have that situation. Instead of believing they can't do it as well as you can, you need to give them some coaching.

One day when I was running a seminar I was watching one of the participants trying to stick a piece of flip-chart paper onto the wall. It was obvious (well it was to me) that he wasn't using enough sticky tape and the paper kept peeling off the wall. In my effort to be helpful (and caring) I said, 'Let me do it for you, I've done this many times before.' As I stuck the paper to the wall he walked away and in a self-mocking, childlike way said to the other participants, 'I'm too stupid to stick a flip chart on a wall.' We all had a good laugh. However, it really made me think about the message I was sending. In my effort to be helpful and caring I was sending a silent message to him that suggested he was stupid and I was much smarter than him. If I'd left him for a few minutes longer, he'd have figured that it needed more tape to stick the paper to the wall and sorted it out himself.

What do you need?

Managers who convey their high expectations to their team have certain characteristics in common that make the Pygmalion effect work to their advantage.

1. They have a high level of self-belief and confidence in what they do.

2. They believe that they can develop the talents of their team by selecting the right people, training them and motivating them.

The Four Factor Theory

Robert Rosenthal identified Four Factors that managers use to convey their expectations.

Climate

This is the mood or spirit created by the manager; the non-verbal behaviour – facial expressions, body language and voice tones. The empowering manager has open and accepting facial expressions and body language. He is not closed and judgemental. The voice tone is reasonable and calm, not loud and demanding or accusing. When you talk to your team members or about others you should never use sarcasm or innuendo.

Feedback

The empowering manager provides regular feedback, with a concentration on Confirming feedback. You need to praise your team members for their initiative and success. When something needs to be improved, empowering managers will make positive suggestions on what to do differently and encourage rather than condemn.

Input

Empowering managers teach their team members what they know; they share information. They don't attempt to retain their position of power by withholding information. They challenge the team members to develop and grow by providing assignments that grow more difficult. They measure their success by the success of their team members and by their continuing growth and development.

Output

Empowering managers encourage their team members to question the way things are done and to suggest new and better ways.

They expect their team members to be proactive in making things better for the team and the organisation's business.

Empowerment is not just some management buzz word that has no meaning for you. It's a highly effective way to motivate your team, get your job done effectively and minimise your stress.

7
Power Listening

Man's inability to communicate is a result of his failure to listen effectively, skilfully and with understanding to another person.

Carl Rogers

THE EARLY DAYS

Let's take a trip down Memory Lane, back to our schooldays. Now, for you, that might not be a long time ago, but for me it was back in the dark ages. Do you remember being taught how to read? You probably even learned the basics of reading before you went to school. Remember all the stuff about, 'The cat sat on the mat'?

Once we'd mastered that we moved on to reading more sophisticated books and I remember most of them being particularly boring; I'm such a Philistine. *Ivanhoe* by Sir Walter Scott was one I remember trying to get my brain around; nowhere as good as the television series I used to watch on children's TV.

My mother used to buy the *Children's Newspaper*. This was to improve my understanding of what was going on in the world and much better than those rubbishy comics that I loved so much; Dan Dare in the *Eagle* was much more interesting.

At school, the teacher would often ask someone in class to read out loud. As well as improving our reading skills it also taught us to speak better. The kids in my class were always being corrected when they mispronounced something or struggled over a particular word.

No one could ever understand what I was saying when it came to my time to read. Throughout my schooldays I wore braces on my teeth. These got in the way of my tongue, causing me to speak like some kind of alien from deep space.

Along with all this reading and speaking, we were also taught to write on lined paper, so neatly and clearly. All this reading, writing and speaking was to ensure we could communicate with the others of our species. However, there's another communication skill that we used a lot and never received any teaching in how to do it, and that was listening.

Listening was probably the communication skill we were introduced to first; as we lay in our cot listening to all the adults cooing and telling us how pretty and clever we were. It's a wonder that we didn't all grow up talking baby talk.

We were never taught to listen, we just experienced it. It's like breathing in and breathing out, like smelling something or seeing something. Nobody teaches you that stuff – you just do it.

However, because we're not taught to listen, most of us don't do it well. We don't in fact listen – we hear.

'Listen' to the facts

> *Power Listening isn't about hearing; it's about really understanding the message that the other person is sending.*

Power Listening isn't about hearing; it's about really understanding the message that the other person is sending and letting them know that you understand and care about what they're saying. That doesn't mean to say that you agree or like what they're saying, only that you really understand. And that's where the difficulty arises.

I could listen all day to someone speaking in Cantonese but I wouldn't understand what they were trying to tell me. (Sometimes I listen to people speaking to me in English and I haven't a clue what they're trying to tell me.)

Now you might consider yourself a good listener but just stop for a moment and think. How would the following people rate you as a listener: your best friend, your boss, your employees, colleagues and even your nearest and dearest? Rather not think about it, eh? Let me give you some facts and figures about listening that have been established by research.

- We spend 45 per cent of our waking time listening, 30 per cent talking, 16 per cent reading and 9 per cent writing.

- We learned to listen first, speaking second, reading third and writing fourth.

- We're taught to listen the least, speak the next least, to read the next most and to write the most.

I hope that hasn't messed up your brain, and I hope you can spot that the communication skill we need the most – listening – is taught the least.

> *The communication skill we need the most – listening – is taught the least.*

As I've said, we spend 45 per cent of our waking time listening. We listen to our families, our work colleagues and our friends. We listen to television, radio, people on the phone and also all the noises that surround us. We probably listen more than we do anything else, except breathing.

Stop reading this for a moment, close your eyes and count the number of different noises you can hear. I'm sitting at my desk in a quiet neighbourhood and I can hear the occasional car passing outside my house. I can hear people speaking as they walk down the street, birds in the trees and some sort of humming noise coming from somewhere; maybe it's the fan in my computer. All of these sounds are competing for space in my brain and that can make it difficult for me to listen to any other incoming message, but more of that later.

More facts and figures: G. R. Bell established in 1984 studies that adults typically practise listening at no better than 25 per cent efficiency. In 1983 G. T. Hunt and A. P. Cusella reported how well training directors in Fortune 500 companies rated the listening effectiveness of managers and subordinates in their organisations. Ratings averaged 1.97 on a five-point scale, somewhere between 'fair' and 'poor.'

Other studies suggest that 60–70 per cent of oral communication is either ignored, misunderstood or quickly forgotten. After 48 hours people are likely to retain less than 25 per cent of what they heard in a conversation.

Now I'm sure this makes a lot of sense to you because one of the most common complaints I hear from managers and employees is, 'My manager doesn't listen to me!'

It's also one of the reasons why difficulties arise in our personal life. How often have people headed for the divorce court saying, 'He never listens to me!' or 'She doesn't understand me!'?

Were we as eloquent as angels we still would please people much more by listening rather than talking.

Charles Caleb Colton (1780–1832, British sportsman writer)

> *Listening is a very powerful management skill. If you want to become a Motivational Manager and minimise your stress then you need to become a Power Listener.*

Listening is a very powerful management skill. If you want to become a Motivational Manager and minimise your stress then you need to become a Power Listener.

I've never been a good listener. However, I work hard at it and I've become a great deal better. So I'm with you on this training exercise to become a Power Listener.

However, it's not just about you as a manager becoming a better listener (and we'll come back to this later). If you bear in mind all the facts and figures we've just looked at, it follows that the members of your team are probably not good listeners. So, you need to take this into consideration when you speak with your team either individually or in a group.

There have been many studies conducted on listening and it's well understood that people only absorb about 10 to 25 per cent of what they hear. Now that may come as a bit of a shock because you probably assume that when you speak with people they *do* understand and remember what you say.

Let's take a look at why people aren't good listeners. As I've just been saying, the first reason is because we haven't been taught. However, there are a whole list of reasons why people don't listen; it's important to be aware, so here are seventeen barriers.

SEVENTEEN BARRIERS TO EFFECTIVE LISTENING

1. It's hard work

Hearing doesn't take any effort; however, listening takes a great deal of concentration and effort. Of course, it gets easier with training and practice, so don't give up on me yet.

> *Hearing doesn't take any effort; listening takes a great deal of concentration and effort.*

2. Distractions

We can be distracted internally and externally. Let's look first at internal distractions.

People have the ability to listen at around 400–700 words per minute. People talk at about 120–150 words per minute. So in any interaction there's a huge amount of brain capacity unused by the listener.

Because we all have so many other things going on in our lives, it's so easy to 'wander off' in our mind and use that surplus brain capacity when someone is speaking to us. We might have personal concerns that pop into our mind such as issues with our partners or children.

Sometimes our thoughts are prompted by the person who's speaking to us. We look at the other person's crushed suit and think, 'I must pop into the dry cleaners on my way home and pick up my suit.'

We're also thinking about our job; people we have to phone, reports we have to write and other people we need to speak to.

We might also just be daydreaming.

And there can be all sorts of external distractions. I speak as someone who is easily distracted. I find it difficult working in an open-plan office. I've been in the situation where I'm listening to someone on the phone and my brain is thinking, 'Who's that person walking past? They must be new here.' 'Look at the state of that guy's suit. Why doesn't he get a new one?' 'Looks like the coffee machine is broken again the way they're all hanging around and kicking it.'

I sometimes used to put my hand over my eyes when listening to customers on the phone. It was the only way I could concentrate on what they were saying.

3. Tiredness

You know you don't listen well when you're tired, so think about this when you're speaking to other people. If they look tired then they may not be listening to everything you're saying.

4. Boredom

People don't listen well when they're not interested or enthused. If the subject is dull to them or the person speaking has a less than enthusiastic monotone voice then the other person stops listening.

5. Out of your comfort zone

If you were to take one of your team away from their place of work and speak to them in your office or the boardroom, then they might feel uncomfortable. If a customer or a client finds themselves in an environment where they feel uncomfortable then they may not listen to you. The trick is to relax people.

6. In a hurry

We're all so busy nowadays with places to go, people to see and things to do. If someone is in a hurry then they're not going to listen well.

7. Know what's being said

This often happens to sales and customer service people. They hear the same comments from customers that they've heard a million times before. The customer only has to say a few words and the sales or customer service person thinks, 'I know what this is about, I've heard it all before', so they stop listening.

It's the same with your team; if they think they know what you're on about, they'll switch off.

8. Not responsible

People will often stop listening if they think they're not responsible for what the other person is saying. They think, 'This is nothing to do with me, I'll just wait till they stop talking or I get a chance to jump in. I'll tell them to speak to somebody else.'

9. Confused

When people don't understand what's being said, they switch off. They'll usually try to understand but after a while they give up and think about something else.

10. Can't make out what's being said

People may not always hear what's being said. However, they don't always communicate this to the speaker. I've been in the situation where I've been spending time with friends in a noisy bar. Someone speaks to me, I don't hear what they've said and I say 'pardon'. They speak again and I still don't hear what they've said.

Sometimes it's the background noise that causes the problem, but also some people speak quite softly. Studies have shown that the female voice can often be difficult to pick up by the male ear.

There are only so many times you can say 'pardon', so I end up trying to pick up certain words and read the body language. However, it has to be said that I'm not really listening.

Sometimes we can't make out what's being said due to the other person's accent. Again, there are only so many times you can say 'pardon'.

It's also important to realise that some people's hearing isn't as good as others. Some people's hearing declines in middle age and again it's not something they want to tell the person who's speaking.

Sometimes people can't make out what's being said because the speaker isn't clear. As I said earlier, there are those with soft voices, however, some people do not have good diction and that makes them difficult to understand. It's also hard to make out if the speaker speaks too fast or too slow.

11. Physically uncomfortable

If people are too hot or too cold or need to visit the loo or they are in any other form of physical discomfort, then they're not going to listen very well.

Good trainers know this and ensure that the training room is as comfortable as possible. They also have lots of breaks for participants to stretch their legs, and allow them to take a 'comfort' break whenever they want.

12. Don't understand the jargon

People will stop listening if the speaker uses jargon or technical language they don't understand. The person listening will even form a dislike for the person using jargon, buzz words or technicalities. The speaker can come across as 'superior' and that can irritate the listener.

I've been in the situation where a speaker uses letters instead of words (I was going to say an acronym but I didn't want to be accused of using 'jargon'). While my brain is working out what the letters mean, the speaker has moved on and effectively I'm not listening.

Over a coffee break in one of my seminars I sat with a group of participants who were managers in a telecom business. They were having a conversation and seemed to speak totally in acronyms: 'I did an MXT yesterday on a VH1 but it developed an XP2.' This conversation went on for about ten minutes and I hadn't a clue what they were talking about. It's okay to use jargon and technical language if the other person understands it. However, I've seen the situation in some organisations where not everyone understands the language. And of course, those who don't understand won't admit it for fear of being perceived as stupid.

13. I'm thinking

It's often the case that people don't listen because they're thinking about what you've just said a few minutes before. You might be briefing one of your team and they start thinking about how they're going to do what you require. The result is that they stop listening and miss the last part of what you say.

Professional speakers and trainers realise this. That's why they often repeat a point later in their session or make the same point in a different way.

I've often been in the situation where a participant at the end of a session asks me a question on something I've answered a short time before. The participant is often met with howls of derision from his colleagues for not listening; however, it's often just the case that the participant was thinking deeply about something that was said earlier.

14. Thinking of what to say next

The next time you're in a social situation and you're telling someone a story about something that's happened to you, watch the other person closely. There often comes a point when they think of a similar thing that happened to them and they start to formulate in their mind how they're going to tell you. They can hardly wait for you to stop talking so they can jump in with their story which is definitely much more interesting than yours. The thing is – they stop listening to you. You can detect the point when they think of their story because their eyes open wider; when you see that, they're not listening anymore.

It has been said, 'People are either speaking or waiting to speak.' If you were giving some Productive feedback to one of your team members about something you were unhappy about then they may not be listening to you. They only want to come back with their side of the story and answer what they think you're on about.

15. Filters get in the way

We all tend to listen through filters that are based on our perceptions, values, experiences and knowledge. We listen auto-biographically based on our view of the world.

To use an extreme example. If someone started to talk about what a wonderful event the Holocaust was, I'm sure many of us would stop listening. Many people would say out loud, 'I'm not listening to this rubbish; this person is a fool.'

This happens all the time in less extreme situations where we filter the information that's being given to us. If we totally disbelieve what someone is telling us or it goes against our understanding, our values and beliefs then we stop listening.

16. We don't like the person who's speaking

People will not listen properly to speakers they don't like or don't trust. They might hear what they say but are reluctant to understand; it's similar to what we said before about listening with filters.

I've seen politicians on TV that I don't particularly like. I'm then very reluctant to listen or give any credibility to what they say. It's highly possible that I'll reach for the remote control and shut them out altogether.

17. We're just not good at listening

We all have different learning styles or ways that we take in information. Some of us are primarily driven by our auditory sense; this means that we are more receptive to what we hear. Others are driven by their visual sense which means that they are more receptive to visual information. And some people are more kinaesthetic, which means that they learn and take in information when they can touch, feel and be involved in something.

Good professional speakers and trainers know this and involve all of the senses in their sessions.

They allow participants to read some text from their workbooks. This is beneficial for the auditory people (reading is about hearing the words inside your head).

They use video or PowerPoint presentations for the visual people.

And they use demonstration, role playing and team discussion for the kinaesthetic people.

I tend to be more visual and kinaesthetic. I really need to be shown something rather than be told about it. My lack of auditory sense means that I'm not particularly interested in music and I don't read for pleasure; I'd much rather watch a film, visit the theatre or go to an art gallery.

This means that people who are not auditory don't tend to be good listeners unless they're shown something. (Can you sense some kind of admission from me?)

That's a heck of a lot of reasons why people don't listen! It's why they don't listen to us and why we don't listen to them.

BENEFITS OF LISTENING

Learning to listen better can absolutely transform your relationships with your team members. Here are three major benefits in developing your listening skills:

1. From a practical business point of view, you learn and find out:

- How the business is doing;
- What your customers are saying and what they really want;
- What your competitors are doing;
- How to save time and work more efficiently;
- How to minimise mistakes and solve problems quickly.

2. **More importantly, from a team motivation point of view you become better at understanding and appreciating:**

- How your team members think and how they feel;
- What goals and ambitions they have;
- The day-to-day challenges they face both business and personal;
- What motivates them.

3. **You develop your motivation skills:**

- By allowing people to relax and open up;
- By building trust;
- By building self-esteem;
- By allowing people to have their say and make their point.
- Listening also compliments the team member.
- It indicates that you value them and think that what they say is important.

EIGHT STEPS TO POWER LISTENING

'Seek first to understand then to be understood'

Stephen Covey, *The Seven Habits of Highly Effective People*

- Actively listen
- Keep an open mind
- Make notes
- Keep eye contact
- Ask questions
- Listen to tone
- Watch body language
- Practise

1. Actively listen

Listening is an active, not a passive, process; in other words, look like you're listening; concentrate completely on the speaker. Express lots of open body language; keep good eye contact; nod your head and change your facial expression relative to what's being said.

Obviously, you don't want to 'go over the top', but merely show your feelings to the other person. Women are good at this and men not so good. The next time you're among a group of people at your place of work or even in a social situation, watch two women or a group talking with each other. You'll see lots of open body language and loads of different facial expression. Without listening in, you could almost tell what the conversation is all about.

Men, on the other hand, tend to listen impassively, just like statues. They may be taking it all in, but the message to the person talking is, 'You're not interested, you don't care and you're probably thinking about something else.' That's often what causes the troubles between couples; women don't get enough visible indications from their men and assume they're not listening (and before you say it – maybe they're not).

And while we're on the subject of the differences in the sexes, be aware that men tend to use direct speech and women indirect.

Let me give you an example of what I mean. Imagine that a couple are driving home from work and she says to him, 'Would you like to stop for a drink?' He interprets this as a direct question and answers, 'No thank you.' They arrive home and he now finds her in a grumpy mood. 'What's wrong?' he asks. 'I wanted to stop for a drink on the way home' she says. 'So why didn't you say so?' says he. 'I did', she says – and so it goes on.

Her question – 'Do you want to go for a drink?' – was her indirect way of saying that she wanted to go for a drink. He interprets it as a direct question and responds accordingly. So if you're listening to someone from the opposite sex, be aware and actively listen.

As well as all the active listening and the open positive body language, make sure you say the occasional.

- 'I see'
- 'Really!'
- 'Uh-huh'
- 'That's great!'
- 'Wow'
- 'I understand'
- 'That's a good point'
- 'I see that you feel strongly about that'.

You've got to work at it to be successful.

2. Keep an open mind

The trap that many people fall into is to allow their own beliefs and perceptions to interfere with what they're hearing.

I often run a listening skills quiz in my seminars and one of the first questions I ask is, 'How many animals of each species did Moses take onto the ark?' I then move on quickly to the next question. Most people believe that I'm asking some kind of trick question. However, they answer question number one with two animals. Of course it was Noah who took the animals onto the ark but that's not what I said. Most people hear part of the story and make a quick decision. It would be difficult for most people to pick up this answer right away but it illustrates the importance of really listening.

During an ice-breaker introduction exercise on one of my recent training workshops, I teamed up with one of the participants. I told him about my background, gave him details of my career to date and my personal circumstances. I explained to him that, although I had lived most of my life in Scotland, there was a spell of six years when I lived in England. He asked me if I liked living in England

and I told him that I did – very much! He seemed slightly surprised at this and asked me again if I really liked living 'south of the border'. I again confirmed this to him and went on to relate how I eventually returned to Scotland to further my career.

This ice-breaker exercise required each of us to tell the others about the person sitting next to us. When my partner started talking about me, he explained fairly clearly about my background. When it came to the episode in my life when I lived in England he said, 'Alan lived in England for six years. However, he didn't like living there and eventually returned to Scotland and found another job.' I was totally taken aback by this statement as it was the total opposite of what I'd said to him.

When we had a moment at the coffee break, I discussed this with him, trying not to cause embarrassment but still wanting to point out his total misrepresentation of what I'd said. After much discussion, we established that what he'd said, he believed to be true. He was sure that I'd said exactly the opposite of what I did say. The only explanation that he could come up with was that he wouldn't like to live in England and couldn't understand why I would like it.

He had heard what I'd told him but his powerful subconscious mind had said, 'No; that's not what Alan means. I know better. He didn't like being in England and that's why he came back to Scotland.'

It can be very difficult to keep an open mind and really listen to what's being said to us. We all have 'filters' in our subconscious through which all incoming information travels and is adjusted to suit our understanding.

Have you ever told a friend something only for them to totally disbelieve you? You tell them that you're going to a pop concert and they say, 'You couldn't possibly like that kind of music!' Or you tell them that you're going to Outer Mongolia on vacation and they say, 'Why on earth would anyone want to go there?'

> *If someone is telling you something, listen hard and accept what they're saying.*

We're all different in how we view the world; so if someone is telling you something, listen hard and accept what they're saying.

3. Make notes

In a social situation it would look a bit strange noting down what people say. However, in a business situation taking notes is very important. It obviously means that you have a record of what's being said. It also tells the person who's speaking that you regard what they say to be important.

Learn the trick of looking at the speaker and writing notes at the same time. It helps if you only write bullet points which are meaningful for you later.

> *Learn the trick of looking at the speaker and writing notes at the same time.*

A friend of mine called in a carpenter to estimate for some refitting work in her house. He walked round with her, made all the right noises, measured things but didn't write anything down. He either had a fantastic memory or he just wasn't interested in the work. It turned out that he did have a good memory; however, my friend didn't give him the job. She felt that he just didn't care enough about her house or his work.

4. Keep eye contact

I've already admitted to not being a great listener. I'm easily distracted by things that go on around me, which is a bit of a challenge when someone is speaking to me. In a business or social situation, I find my eyes wandering, particularly when the person speaking is less than interesting. It is rude, it doesn't help you make a positive impression on the other person and it certainly won't help you become a Motivational Manager.

You need to look at people when they're speaking. Don't stare and make them uncomfortable but keep your eyes on their eyes, only looking away briefly and occasionally.

> *You need to look at people when they're speaking.*

5. Ask questions

This is another good listening technique. Occasionally, and politely, interrupt the person speaking to clarify something they've just said. They won't normally object and it helps check your level of understanding. It also tells the other person that you're deeply interested in what they're saying. This is sometimes called 'paraphrasing', as you're taking 'chunks' of what's been said and repeating it back. You are summarising facts and figures.

Asking questions is also an excellent way of taking control when the other person is starting to ramble and talk too much.

6. Listen to tone

We are all fairly good at picking up on a person's tone of voice and most of us realise that the tone will ultimately decide the meaning of the words.

Picture this scenario: You return home one evening and ask the person you share your life with, 'Have you had a good day?' 'Yesssss,' they reply grumpily. So you then say, 'Has something upset you?' 'Noooo,' they say, again grumpily.

We all know that in this situation, 'Yes' means 'No' and 'No' means 'Yes'. The person we're speaking to may want to cover up the fact that they've had a bad day or they don't want to talk about it or perhaps you've done something wrong and they don't want to tell you.

The point is, you will believe their tone of voice before you believe the words they've used. More often the tone can be very subtle, so you need to listen closely to pick up on a meaning.

Many people don't pick up on what people really mean and often give an inappropriate response. The Motivational Manager develops this skill and works hard to ensure an understanding of what people really are saying.

7. Watch body language

Do you think your ears are the main instruments of listening? Wrong! It's your eyes. Observing body language tells you so much about how a person is feeling and often what they really mean.

If you ask one of your team how they are and they reply, 'Fine thank you', it's going to be a bit hard to believe if their face looks miserable and their body language is slumped in a dejected manner.

Body language will usually confirm or contradict what is being said.

> *Body language will usually confirm or contradict what is being said.*

A business colleague of mine recently attended a seminar where the speaker spoke of his success and about everything he had achieved. My friend was, to a certain extent, impressed by what the speaker was saying. However, he couldn't understand why he was wearing such poor shoes. The speaker's shoes looked cheap, were a bit down at heel and could have done with a polish. If this speaker was so successful, then why couldn't he afford a decent pair of shoes?

Maybe the speaker was as successful as he said he was. However, he was sending out a mixed message.

> *People tend to believe what they see rather than what they hear.*

People tend to believe what they see rather than what they hear.

If you are to become a Power Listener, take into account what you see in the other person but don't fall into any traps. Body language does send out many messages. However, we need to become skilled in understanding what these messages really mean. It's such an important area of human communication and we're going to look at it again later in the book.

8. Practise

Commit to practising your listening skills every day. Whenever you come into contact with someone, be it in business or socially, really listen to that person. It's like any other skill, the more you practise the better you'll become. (And just think how much you will learn.)

So here are the key points for Power Listening:

- **Listen logically** – stay emotionally detached and listen for facts, ideas and details.

- **Stimulate the speaker** – nod your head, lean forward and concentrate totally.

- **Make notes** – get all the details down.

- **Shut out distractions** – change your environment or shut out all distractions in your mind.

- **Listen between the lines for hidden meanings** – listen to the emotional meaning of the speaker, use your intuition and trust your gut feeling.

- **Observe non-verbal clues** – listen for what people are not saying.

- **Listen for what people would like to say** – but have difficulty putting into words.

- **Don't pre-judge** – keep an open mind.

- **Don't interrupt** or jump in with an answer or solution.

THE SECRET LANGUAGE

The Motivational Manager needs to be a Power Listener. However, it's also important to be aware that the people who are listening to you may not be doing it particularly well. So if you want to get your message across then it's important to take into account all the points above, particularly 6 and 7.

In 6 and 7 the point was made that tone of voice and 'listening' to body language are vitally important. The words we use, although essential, can be contradicted by our tone and our body language.

Many people are now familiar with the results of research conducted by Dr Albert Mehrabian. This tell us that the impact of a message is dependent 7 per cent on the words we use, 38 per cent on tone of voice and a whopping 55 per cent on body language.

I've read articles that take issue with these figures, suggesting that words are more important and have greater impact than Dr Mehrabian suggests.

I wouldn't be prepared to put any figures on these three aspects of communication. However, I am totally convinced that how you look and how you sound are far more important than what you say.

> *How you look and how you sound are far more important than what you say.*

Recently I conducted a one-to-one training session in selling skills for a director of a small computer software company. A video camera was used to record this director's sales pitch to a potential customer, a role played by me. When I replayed this recording, my director client was horrified to watch his presentation. In his pitch he used words such as, 'Young exciting company – staff with lots of enthusiasm for their product – lots of energy and passion for what they are doing.' The only thing was that he, the person in the video, had about as much excitement, enthusiasm, energy and passion as a plate of cold porridge.

He was saying the words but they just weren't convincing. He was dull, monotone and boring, and he knew it. The good thing was that once he'd realised it, he could do something about it.

On occasion people say to me, 'I am as I am, I'm a quieter sort of person. I can't leap up and down and get excited about something even though I feel it inside.'

My answer to these people is, 'Don't change your personality but do make a slight change to your behaviour. Turn up the energy a little bit, put a bit more power in the enthusiasm, and warm up the passion just a tad more.'

If you were to ask these same people about their football team, their children or their hobby, just watch them get fired up or at least get a little bit warmer.

One quiet unassuming chap held me spellbound one day telling me about his hobby of beekeeping. It wasn't so much what he was saying but how he was describing it. His eyes were shining, he was speaking quickly and he was using his hands to describe this subject which he had now made very interesting.

> *If you want to get your message across to your team members, show more of how you feel.*

So if you want to get your message across to your team members, show more of how you feel. Other people will respond more to your feelings than to what you actually say.

More secret language

The point has now been well made that it's not what we say that influences other people but more how we say it. Non-verbal communication is so powerful and we can use it much more to our advantage; this doesn't mean in a manipulative way but more in a way that builds rapport with your team members.

People 'buy' people first and they tend to buy people who are very much like themselves. Now, you can't become exactly like any member of your team. However, you can make slight adjustments to your behaviour that will build rapport and improve communication.

Let's say that you have a fairly strong voice or you speak fairly quickly. If you're communicating with someone in the team who has a soft voice or another team member who speaks slowly, then they may feel you're a rather different person from them and they may even feel intimidated. The obvious answer is either to talk with a soft voice or speak more slowly.

This technique is known as 'mirroring' and it basically means behaving as closely as you can to the other person. Speak at the same level they do, speak at the same speed and with the same tone. This doesn't mean mimicking the other person – this would quickly switch them right off you. It's about subtly becoming more like the other person.

You can also learn to mirror words and phrases, posture, eye contact, facial expression and hand gestures. Some people say they feel uncomfortable doing this; however, they often mirror people unconsciously. Just watch someone talking to a small child or a baby. They crouch down to the child's level, they put a soft smile on their face and they talk in a childlike way. If we can do it with children, then we can do it with adults, particularly if you want them to accept you and what you say.

Many people believe that to be a Motivational Manager you need to be a good speaker: in fact, you need to be a *great* listener!

> *Many people believe that to be a Motivational Manager you need to be a good speaker: in fact, you need to be a* great *listener!*

8
Problems can be a problem

BE CAREFUL HOW YOU SPEND YOUR TIME

Do you remember when you first became a manager? You probably inherited a team of people who came with all sorts of problems for you to resolve. It made you feel so important having all these people who needed you to solve their problems large or small.

After all, that was why you were promoted into a managerial role – you knew the business, knew the customers and had vast experience of handling problems. I'm sure there were lots of other reasons for giving you the job. However, dealing with problems has always been seen as part of the job. But don't you sometimes get a bit fed up with having to solve all these problems?

My first job in management was as a regional sales manager in charge of six fields sales engineers. This was in the days before mobile phones so the guys used to phone me at home in the evenings. At first I would let them phone me anytime because I wanted to be 'there for them'. I was their leader and I thought they couldn't survive without me.

However, when I was getting phone calls just as I was about to tuck into some well-deserved dinner, changes had to be made. So we agreed on a time window when I could be phoned and that worked okay for a while. However, I started to get sick and tired of these problems eating into my personal life. It wasn't the case that the six of them would phone me every night but some would phone more than others and some would demand more time on the phone. At that time I didn't know what to do about it, so it was tolerated – it was just part of the job.

I was eventually promoted to an office-based sales manager job and there were even more problems to be dealt with. It wasn't just the sales guys I had to deal with; it was the people from the finance department, the marketing department, the distribution people, and of course the customers.

I remember when I took my first week's holiday from this job and thinking before my return to work, 'My desk will be piled up with problems to be solved, there will be people standing in line at the door of my office waiting for me to solve their problems.' The funny thing was, there weren't as many problems as I'd thought there would be.

Solving problems *is* part of your job as a Motivational Manager. Do it well and you'll have a happy and motivated team. Do it badly or spend too much time dealing with problems and you'll have exactly the opposite.

> *Solving problems is part of your job as a Motivational Manager. Do it well and you'll have a happy and motivated team. Do it badly or spend too much time dealing with problems and you'll have exactly the opposite.*

In Chapter 4 we looked at spending quality time with your team, listening, giving feedback and coaching them. One of the reasons some managers don't do this well is because **they spend too much time solving business problems.**

I'm sad to say that some managers like solving business problems. They see it as a major part of their job and it makes them feel important and worthwhile.

However, while a manager is sitting at his desk solving problems, the listening, feedback and coaching isn't getting done. And if that isn't getting done, you're in danger of creating a demotivated team who take too many sickies and don't make a positive contribution to your business.

So we need to look at the whole situation of dealing with problems.

Most people spend more time and energy going around problems than in trying to solve them.

Henry Ford (1863–1947, American industrialist, founder of Ford Motor Company)

BUSINESS PROBLEMS – PEOPLE PROBLEMS

If you want to be a successful Motivational Manager, you need to minimise your time spent solving business problems and focus on any people problems you may have with your team.

This book isn't about time management, so I suggest you get hold of a book on the subject or attend a training course and take a long hard look at how you spend your time.

> *Your success as a Motivational Manager will be determined by the amount of time you spend with your team.*

Your success as a Motivational Manager will be determined by the amount of time you spend with your team. If you're faced with too many business problems then I suggest you have a meeting with your boss. If you need any help in this area, go back to Chapter 5 and have a look at where we talked about giving feedback to your boss. You need to make the case that business problems get in the way of managing your team and therefore jeopardise your ability to achieve your objectives.

I remember one day, just as I was about to leave the office to spend some time with one of my sales people making calls on customers, my boss, the Sales Director, stopped me to suggest I join him at a meeting to discuss how we could solve some problems in the administration process.

Now that would have been the easiest thing in the world for me to do; sit in on another meeting and possibly prove to the people there what a clever chap I was. However, I resisted the temptation to give in to my manager's request and said, 'My plan is to spend some valuable time with our salesman, John, helping him to increase his sales conversion rate and so bring more sales into the business. Are you telling me you don't want me to do that and instead attend this meeting?' There wasn't much he could say about that other than to suggest I continue with my plan to spend time with John.

I'm not saying that I won every one of these discussions; sometimes I was overruled and made to do what the boss wanted. However, my prime objective as a Motivational Manager was to achieve my outcomes through the efforts of my team. Attending meetings and solving business problems wasn't going to do that.

Fight hard for the time you spend with your people, that time will determine your success.

A man must be master of his hours and days, not their servant.

William Frederick Book

RECOGNISING PEOPLE PROBLEMS

As a Motivational Manager you need to determine what problems exist with your people and if these problems warrant your time and energy. Before you decide to act on any potential people problems you need to establish four things:

1. Does a problem exist?

2. What kind of problem is it?

3. Whose problem is it?

4. What actions should you take?

Does a problem exist?

You need to be really sure that you do have a people problem. Do you remember in Chapter 2 where I talked about how I used to get angry when a member of my team showed up late for a meeting or an appointment with me? My anger was primarily a reaction to my programming. I was brought up to believe that it was important to be on time; however, **is it a problem?**

Is it a problem if one of your team:

- Isn't a good team player?
- Is a bit overweight?
- Doesn't complete reports on time?
- Isn't a good writer or speller?
- Is always late?
- Has bad breath?
- Is a sloppy dresser?
- Is a bit negative?

I can't answer any of these questions – only you can.

I once had a salesman on my team called Brian who, to my mind, had a strange taste in clothes. He was always clean and tidy but his hair was a bit long for my liking and he wore too much male jewellery. Again, the manner in which I reacted to his appearance was all down to my inbuilt programmes, the way I saw the world. However, what he did do was bring in the sales. The customers liked him, he always hit his target and so, I achieved my outcomes.

It would have been easy for me to allow Brian's appearance to become a problem. Trying to resolve this problem, by getting Brian to dress in a way that I thought was more appropriate, would have had negative consequences. I would have been in great danger of demotivating Brian and affecting his ability to bring in the sales.

In order to determine if a problem exists, consider these four points:

1. Think, don't react.

2. Can you do anything about it?

3. Is it worth doing anything about it?

4. You can't make people what they're not.

Think, don't react

Remember what I said in Chapter 2 about the first Factor of Success: 'Successful managers have a deep understanding of their own minds. They're aware of their needs, their strengths and weaknesses, and their emotions. They're honest with themselves and with their team members. You have to decide who runs your mind. Is it you or is it somebody else?'

Don't react to any inbuilt program about how people should behave. Don't allow something to become a problem that isn't a problem. Getting angry and stressed isn't good for your health and is not a productive way to motivate your team.

Can you do anything about it?

If, for example, one of your team is a bit overweight and you think it's a problem, can you really do anything about it? I don't think so.

Is it worth doing anything about it?

Again, it's back to thinking and not reacting. Ask yourself, 'Is this perceived problem affecting my ability to achieve my outcomes?' The answer will tell you if you have a problem or not.

You can't make people what they're not

Don't waste your time trying to change people who can't be changed. Some managers still believe that if they see a perceived weakness or problem with a team member then they can be changed. They send them on training courses, tell them what to do, threaten them with disciplinary action or the sack and then wonder why there's no change. The Motivational Manager concentrates on developing the strengths of team members, not trying to correct their 'weaknesses'.

Let me summarise: if you want to know if a problem exists, ask yourself, 'Does this "problem" affect my outcomes, goals, objectives, targets or whatever I'll be judged on?'

If it does have negative consequences for your outcomes, then you have a problem.

WHAT KIND OF PROBLEM IS IT?

Once you've determined that you really do have a problem with a member of your team, you need to determine what kind of problem it is. Knowing what kind of problem it is will enable you to decide the best course of action to resolve it. Typical problems could be:

- Unable to bring in the sales;
- Unable to handle a difficult customer;
- Unable to get reports in on time;
- Unable to do the job quickly enough;
- Keeps making mistakes;
- Upsets customers.

There are four factors to consider:

1. Is this the right person for the job?

2. Do they have the skills to do the job?

3. Are they motivated to do the job?

4. Is there some other factor?

Let's look at each of these in turn.

Is this the right person for the job?

You may have inherited a team member or you may have selected them yourself. However, you'll have to 'bite the bullet' and decide whether or not they are the right person for the job.

I've experienced customer service people who shouldn't be let anywhere near a customer, secretarial assistants who couldn't spell or type fast enough, engineers who couldn't read blueprints and plumbers who couldn't plumb.

A telecoms manager on one of my seminars was telling me about one of his engineers who worked in the tunnels under London maintaining cables and equipment. This guy was always off sick, and when he was at work he kept making mistakes and generally not doing his job very well. The engineer had been spoken to on several occasions about his poor performance; however, he hadn't made much progress. Eventually they discovered that he suffered from claustrophobia. He was trying to deal with it himself and didn't want to tell anyone as he thought he would be perceived as weak and not able to do the job like the rest of his mates. He was obviously in the wrong job and was immediately transferred to another role where he wouldn't have to work in enclosed spaces.

A client of mine realised that the customer service person they'd recently employed couldn't handle the pressure of difficult customers and situations. They realised that training wouldn't solve the situation, so they transferred her to a job where she produced quotations and didn't have to speak to a customer.

In the opening chapter of this book I told you about apprentice engineers who worked with me in my first job. These guys went through all the training that I went through but some of them found it really tough. There was no way that these people would ever be successful engineers and hopefully they all found a career more suitable to their talents.

> *If you have someone in your team who is unable to do the job and is unable to learn, then you need to transfer them into something they can do or advise and help them to find other employment.*

If you have someone in your team who is unable to do the job and is unable to learn, then you need to transfer them into something they can do or advise and help them to find other employment. Now I know that may seem harsh and it's not always easy or feasible to release people. However, you'll never achieve your outcomes with the wrong person in the job. The business may suffer and you're in great danger of demotivating the other members of your team. They won't want someone on the team who can't do the job.

Do they have the skills to do the job?

There are organisations that are excellent at training people to do the job they employ them to do. Sadly, there are many others who don't effectively train people to do their job.

There was one company I joined after three years' experience in selling. They had a first-class induction training programme. I spent the first two weeks on a residential training course learning all about the products. They went into fine detail and regularly tested me on my product knowledge.

The second two weeks were spent 'in the field' calling on customers with a field sales trainer. The next two weeks were spent back in the training school, learning how to sell the products. I learned a great deal about selling with this company and it gave me a great deal of confidence when I was left to 'fly solo'.

Funnily enough, they weren't as good at managing their people as I first believed and as a result suffered a huge turnover of sales people. I certainly learned a lot about selling from this organisation. However, I also learned a lot about how not to manage people. This stood me in good stead when it came my time to step up to management.

However, as I said earlier, too many organisations don't even train their people well enough to do the job. I've known sales organisations that employ experienced sales people and expect them to sell the new product or service with very little product knowledge training or awareness of the new market in which they're working. They seem to believe that if a sales person has experience and has been trained in selling, then they'll have all the attributes needed to do the job.

I've also known organisations employ really smart and articulate customer service people but not give them enough training in the product or the service or the industry they'll be working in.

If you have an issue with an individual who isn't performing the way you need them to, you need to consider carefully if they have a skill problem. Perhaps the job has changed since they were employed and their skills haven't been updated.

> *If you have an issue with an individual who isn't performing the way you need them to, you need to consider carefully if they have a skill problem.*

Remember, your team members may not want to admit to not having the skill to do a job. Some people aren't comfortable telling you that they don't know what to do. They don't want to be perceived as stupid in front of you or their colleagues.

Spend some quality time

In Chapter 3 I put great emphasis on the need to spend quality time with your team. This is absolutely vital if you want to identify the cause of problems or spot them before they happen.

A client company of mine was having problems with underperforming sales people. I quickly established that the area managers spent very little time with the field sales people. They tended to manage their teams from behind a desk, analysing sales reports and other data.

The area manager would occasionally sit down with each sales person and go through these reports. The manager would look at each customer report in turn and question the sales person on why a sale had been lost.

The sales team basically saw it as a 'find fault' exercise; they hated it, it demotivated them and the message from the manager was, 'Get it sorted.'

When I was a field sales manager I used to spend a great deal of my time with my sales people, calling on customers. This gave me lots of opportunities to 'catch people doing something right' and give them some Confirming feedback. It also gave me the opportunity to give some Productive feedback if I observed something I wasn't so happy about. I was able to monitor at first hand how things could be done better. I could also see where mistakes were being made, which might lead to problems at a later stage and possibly a loss in sales.

Spending time with one of my team away from the customers, over lunch or a drink after work, gave me the opportunity to identify any human problems they might be having. If they were experiencing some problems at home with their partner or family, then this could obviously cause problems at work. There may not be much you can do about these problems, but at least you can show your understanding and be supportive of the individual.

Susan worked on my telesales team a few years back and she used to make a lot of simple mistakes when processing a customer's order. After observing her for a short period of time, it dawned on me what was happening. At the end of each call to a customer, there was a process of completing the customer's order details on the computer. I noticed that Susan was easily distracted by other things going on in the office. She was always jumping from her seat to help her colleagues or anyone who came into the office. Susan was a really lovely person, always looking to be helpful. The problem was, she would speak to someone or leave her desk in the middle of processing a transaction. The result was that things would get missed out and mistakes made.

I spent time coaching Susan to complete each transaction before doing anything else or speaking to anyone. I just had to improve Susan's skill in handling a transaction.

Let's consider another example. Say one of your team isn't producing reports fast enough. There's no point telling them to work faster or 'buck up' their ideas. Perhaps you to need to send them on a training course in how to use Microsoft Word or Excel or whatever programme they're using.

If you have a skill problem with a member of your team, don't regard them as a no-hoper. Coach them on the job or organise some external training.

Are they motivated to do the job?

Sometimes an employee is labelled as having the wrong attitude to do the job. It's acknowledged that they're the right person for the job and they certainly don't lack training. However, they just don't seem motivated.

Some years ago when computers started to become an integral part of many jobs, some organisations encountered problems with certain employees. They were heard to say, 'These computers are a waste of time, I'd rather do it the old way' or 'There's no way I'm using a computer' or 'I hear that computers make mistakes and give you even more problems' or 'This is a complete waste of money.'

On hearing these comments, some managers would accuse the employee of being negative and having the wrong attitude, of living in the past, not thinking of the good of the company and not being motivated to do the job.

These responses from managers may be true but perhaps there was another reason for the negative comments.

It was found that once the dissenters had been trained to use the computers, they often became their strongest advocates. In other words, it wasn't a motivation problem, it was a training problem that could be easily resolved.

Sometimes when employees are faced with a new job, a new task or a different way of doing things, they may appear negative and lacking in motivation. However, they may just be afraid or insecure about taking on a new task, not being able to do it and making a fool of themselves. And of course, if you're not spending quality time with them, then they're unlikely to share their concerns with you.

I had a client who had difficulty sending some of her female team members on my two-day residential training course. As mothers, they were citing children commitments as a reason not to attend the course. The manager offered to resolve the childcare issues but still met with resistance from some of her team. She put it down to a bad attitude and a lack of motivation.

However, more thorough investigation may have identified what the real problem was. Perhaps the team members had a fear of training courses, of meeting new people or even staying in a hotel. They may even have had a spouse who didn't want them staying away from home overnight. And of course, it may just have been a problem with childcare.

There could be a way around these sorts of concerns, possibly by reassuring the team members that they won't feel threatened on the training course. You may even wish to phone their spouse and discuss the situation with them.

Again, you may not be able to resolve these issues but your greater understanding and willingness to listen will improve your status as a Motivational Manager.

Sometimes you will encounter a motivation problem when a team member is 'punished' for doing the job well. Have you ever heard the saying, 'If you want a job done well, give it to a busy person'? This often happens in an organisation when an employee does a job well and is always busy getting on with it. People then give them more work or responsibility because they know they will do it well. However, the employee gets over-loaded with work and starts to get demotivated.

That's why it's so important to spend quality time with every member of your team, not just the poor performers. People who are overloaded with work may not always tell you, perhaps because they don't want to appear as a whinger. Nonetheless, they are in danger of becoming seriously demotivated. Spend time with them and assess their workload. If it's too much, find someone else to do it.

There's another reason why you may think you a have a motivation problem with a team member. Sometimes people don't perform well or appear demotivated just to get your attention. Now I appreciate that this is a situation that some managers find difficulty in getting their head around. However, it does happen. We looked at acknowledgement in Chapter 4 and the fact that some people may behave badly in order to get your attention.

I've been in the situation where I've spent time with one of my team trying to find out what's wrong with them and why they're demotivated. They come up with all sorts of issues that seem trivial and we go round and round these issues not getting anywhere. I end up thinking, 'What's wrong with this person? I can't understand them and I don't know what to do with them!'

All the time I spent with them may just have been satisfying their need for acknowledgement. The issues they raised were trivial and there wasn't any real answer to them, so I needed to try another approach.

I eventually found that it was better not to concentrate on why they were demotivated; it was far better to concentrate on all the things they did well. So I made sure that I 'caught them doing something right' as often as I could and gave them lots of Confirming feedback.

Of course, it has to be said that if you've been using all the skills we've covered previously in the book, you're going to have fewer motivational problems in the first place.

Is there some other factor?

Even if your team members are motivated and willing to do the job, you may still experience people problems if they suffer from a lack of resources, such as they:

- Don't have the right equipment to do the job;

- Don't have much support from colleagues;

- Don't have enough time to do the job;

- Don't have the right environment to do the job;

- Feel they don't earn enough money.

I mentioned earlier about a telesales team I inherited and how I faced the challenge of turning around this underperforming team. I appointed Christine as the team leader and manager and I wanted her to spend more time coaching people on the job. However, this wasn't getting done to my satisfaction and I realised I needed to spend more time with Christine, coaching *her*. When discussing with Christine how she spent her day, it became apparent that there was one task that took up nearly two hours of her time. It was a credit control procedure that required Christine to check all the orders coming in and resolve credit issues. I asked Christine, 'Why do you do that job?' 'Because I've always done it, its part of my job.' 'Do you like doing it?' 'No, it's a real pain, I see myself as a team leader and coach, not a credit control person.' 'Do you think it should be done by the credit control department?' 'Yes of course it should, and they could probably do it a lot better and quicker than me.'

So the next day I had a meeting with the credit control manager and he responded, 'Yes you're right. Christine shouldn't be doing that job; it's a historical situation and should really be dealt with in the credit control department. Transfer that function to my department and we'll deal with it from now on.'

Overnight Christine found herself with two hours extra in her day; time that could be valuably spent coaching her team members and bringing in more sales.

I accept that not all resource problems are so easily resolved. However, your job is to spend time with your team and minimise the number of obstacles that get in the way of them doing their job.

There are many resource problems that you won't be able to do anything about. For example, it's not always easy to get a team member more money. However, if they have money problems then you may be able to get them some professional advice. Many organisations have support procedures within their human resources department.

Some other resource problems can be dealt with by reframing. Let me give you an example. One team of sales people that I managed felt they had a big problem in achieving their sales targets because our two major competitors did so much television advertising. Our company had 14 per cent of the market for our product and the two main competitors had approximately 40 per cent each. They had a huge TV advertising budget and we had virtually nil.

I reframed the situation for my team explaining how we could develop our business in a more exclusive niche market than our high-volume competitors. I used the analogy of the car industry; BMW aren't as big or sell as many cars as Ford, but that doesn't mean their product isn't as good.

Sometimes a team member will feel that they aren't receiving enough support from other departments in the organisation. This may be true and it's your job to do your best to resolve any problems with other departments. It may be tempting to ignore the problem and hope it goes away, and you may or may not be able

Spending time discussing concerns will show the team member that you care; it's all about treating each member of your team as a valued and respected person.

to do anything about it. However, you need to demonstrate to your team that you are doing whatever it takes to resolve these problems. If unsuccessful, you need to use all the motivational skills described before. Spending time discussing concerns will show the team member that you care; it's all about treating each member of your team as a valued and respected person.

Keep giving Confirming feedback and outweigh the negative feelings that result from a lack of resources.

WHOSE PROBLEM IS IT?

Being unclear about who owns the problem is a trap that many managers fall into. As I said earlier, some managers spend too much time solving problems and don't do enough of the valuable feedback and coaching.

So when a problem arises, be it a business or people problem, ask yourself, 'Whose problem is it? Is it mine or is it the team member's?'

Say, for example, one of your team, Jane, was complaining that she hadn't received her bonus or her expenses. You're aware that all bonus and expense claims have to be submitted by the 12th of the month. You also know that Jane isn't very good at getting her claims in on time. It would be so easy to accept this as your problem. You may think it motivational to resolve this for Jane, so you decide to phone the HR department or whoever deals with salaries and get Jane's bonus organised. This may take a short amount of your time or it may take longer; however long it is, it's too long. This is not your problem. It's Jane's and it's up to her to resolve it.

Let me give you a definition of a problem: A problem is the difference between actual conditions and those that are required or desired. The problem belongs to the person who is unable or unwilling to accept the negative consequences of these differences.

Okay, so that might be a bit heavy, but the point is: does the problem above have negative consequences for your outcomes or for Jane?

Let me give you another example from personal life. Have you ever heard a mother say of her son, 'Bob's hopeless in the kitchen. If he didn't have someone to look after him and cook his meals, he'd starve'? Of course, Bob probably would starve. Why? Because his mother always cooked for him. When Bob said he didn't know how to boil an egg, his mother did it for him instead of coaching him how to do it himself.

If you continue to 'solve' problems for your team members, they will keep expecting you to do it.

> *If you continue to 'solve' problems for your team members, they will keep expecting you to do it.*

Let's look at four examples and decide whose problem they are.

1. Mark, one of my sales team, came to me one day with a tale of woe: 'Those people in the accounts department are making life difficult for me. They're really unhelpful and they're stopping me from doing my job. You'll have to do something about it Alan.'

2. Christine, the telesales manager I mentioned earlier, phoned me one day: 'The team are complaining about Joan; she has really bad body odour and it's affecting the morale in the office. What are you going to do about it Alan?'

3. David, another of my team, comes to me with two proposals that he's going to put forward to a new customer. He lays them on my desk and says, 'Which of these should I offer to the customer Alan?'

4. John, another field salesman, tells me, 'This new product won't sell on my area. I know it sells on other areas but there's no market for it on mine, my customers are different. I think you have a problem with it Alan.'

In Example 1, is it my problem or is it Mark's? It's Mark's. He wants me to talk with the manager in the accounts department and tell him to make sure his people are more helpful to Mark. That just isn't feasible. It will only get people annoyed in the accounts department and it won't resolve the issue.

In Example 2, is it my problem or is it Christine's? It's Christine's. She wants me to speak to Joan about her BO problem; however, Christine is Joan's manager, not me.

In Example 3, is it my problem or David's? It's David's. He wants me to make a decision that will affect one of his customers. However, David is in possession of all the facts and I'm not. He was best placed to make the decision.

In Example 4 is it my problem or John's? It's mine. John is having difficulty selling this product. I know it sells on other areas and John's lack of sales will have a direct effect on me achieving my targets, so it is my problem.

I'm not suggesting you ignore problems 1, 2 and 3. However, you must not fall into the trap of taking these problems on board and accepting them as your own.

> *Clearly identifying whose problem something is has a fundamental effect on your success as a Motivational Manager.*

Clearly identifying whose problem something is has a fundamental effect on your success as a Motivational Manager. It's not just about you freeing up time to do other things or avoiding nasty jobs; it's about making decisions that will have a positive effect on your team.

When it's your problem

Let's look at what we need to do when it's the manager's problem, as in Example 4. You need to find a solution by talking with the person involved. We looked at giving feedback in Chapter 5 and the point was made about the importance of using 'I' messages and not 'you' messages. So let's see how that would work in Example 4. It could give me more problems if I was to say to John:

- You're not selling hard enough.

- You're not pulling your weight.

- You've got some kind of problem with this product.

- You'd better do something about your lack of sales.

- You're not trying hard enough.

- You should know better.

- You've let me down.

If I was to approach it this way, I'm more likely to annoy John. He might just switch off and he certainly wouldn't be motivated to go out and get more sales. There would be resistance, resentment and possibly total submission.

It's better to use 'I' messages such as:

- I'm unwilling to accept the level of sales in your area.

- I'm unhappy about your lack of sales.

- I'm willing to talk this through with you.

- I believe, between us, we can work this through.

I would then go on to ask John about any suggestions he might have for improving his sales. If he was unable to come up with anything, then I'd make some suggestions and ask him to come up with the best course of action. We would then agree the course of action and the date when we'd review the situation.

The Motivational Manager gets the team member involved in the decision making process; he gets their buy-in.

> *The Motivational Manager gets the team member involved in the decision making process.*

When it's their problem

When the problem is a team member's, walking away isn't an option; as a Motivational Manager you need to help them find the answer to their problem. You need to help them understand that the problem is theirs and that they accept responsibility for solving it. Listen to what the problem is and:

- Ask lots of questions;

- Keep listening, empathise: 'I don't like that when it happens to me';

- Ask them what they think they should do; what are the options?

- Ask them what the result of each option would be;

- Ask what other solutions might work.

In Example 1 I asked Mark to give me the full story and I asked further questions based on what he said:

- Who, specifically, are the people you have a problem with in this department?

- What exactly is it that they say or do that gives you a problem?

- How do you think you could approach this in future?

- Do you think you could use any of your sales skills to solve this problem?

- What will be your next step?

In Example 2, I explained to Christine that as she was Joan's manager, it was her problem to resolve. I then asked her how she proposed to deal with it:

- How would she approach Joan?

- What would she say? What words would she use?

- How did she think Joan would react?

- How would she respond to what Joan said?

- What suggestions would she make if asked?

- Did she think 'I' messages would be better than 'you' messages?

In Example 3, I asked David:

- What options were best for his customer's needs?

- What did he think was the best option?

- Why did he think this was the best option?

- Was this also the best option for our business – win-win?

In Examples 1, 2 and 3, helping the individual to solve their own problem is hugely motivational for them.

Problem of conflict in the team

You may come up against a problem where two members of your team are in conflict. For example, Mary comes to you and says, 'I'm not happy working beside Joe. He's always telling me what to do, he's in my face and he criticises how I deal with customers. He's a real pain and I want you to move me away from him.'

You know it isn't possible to move Mary and you know it's not your problem – it's Mary's. You need to respond as shown previously, when we looked at 'When it's their problem'.

Explain to Mary about 'I' messages and 'you' messages and encourage her to sit down with Joe to try to resolve the situation. If that doesn't work and you feel it's affecting team morale and your ability to achieve your outcomes, then you may have to take the following steps:

- Agree to sit down with them both at a specific time for a specific time;

- Ask them both to write down what the problems are and the options for solving the problems;

- Ask them both at the meeting to read their points and get an agreement on what the problem really is;

- Discuss each point and ask what is or isn't acceptable to them;

- Identify which option has the least disagreement and agree to make it work;

- Set a time to review the situation.

As I've said before, you won't win them all but if you don't take any action you won't win any.

Your job is to solve both business and people problems, and doing this the right way will increase your skill as a Motivational Manager.

9
Give Them What They Want

WHAT DO THEY WANT?

What do people actually want from their work? What is it that really motivates them?

What is it that gets them out of bed in the morning and makes them reasonably happy to go to work and do a good job?

You might be thinking, 'It's different for each individual', and you're probably right. There is no such thing as a simple all-encompassing solution and that's not going to make your job as a Motivational Manager any easier.

In Chapters 4, 5 and 6 we looked at three factors that I like to call The Three Secrets of Team Motivation.

1. Spend quality time;

2. Give feedback and coach;

3. Be a believer.

My experience of managing teams tells me that spending quality time with each person, giving Confirming and Productive feedback and believing and empowering them will make a massive contribution to motivation at work. Of course, I've said it

> *Spending quality time with each person, giving Confirming and Productive feedback and believing and empowering them will make a massive contribution to motivation at work.*

before and I'll say it again: 'You don't motivate people at work. You create the environment in which they motivate themselves.'

As well as The Three Secrets of Team Motivation, there are other factors you need to take into consideration if you want to make people happy at work.

Let's look at some of the motivation theories that have been around for several years. As I've said before, I'm a very practical manager and I only want to give you information that will make your life easier. However, I believe that it's important to understand these theories and how they might affect you. I'm sure you will have heard of some, if not all, of them. Nevertheless, here's my understanding of their influence on the day-to-day working environment.

THEORY X AND THEORY Y

In 1960 Douglas McGregor, an American social scientist, published his book The Human Side of Enterprise. In it he examined theories on the behaviour of individuals at work and formulated two models, theory x and theory y. He advanced the idea that managers had a major part in motivating staff and he divided them into the two categories.

Theory x managers (authoritarian management style) believe that:

- Their staff are lazy, dislike work and will avoid it if they can;

- Their staff prefer to be directed and dislike responsibility;

- Their staff need explicit instructions and need to be threatened if they don't do what they're supposed to do;

- Their staff are relatively unambitious and want security above all else.

Theory y managers (participative management style) believe that:

- Their staff really want to do their best at work;

- Their work is as natural as play or rest;

- Staff will direct themselves if committed to the objective of the organisation;

- Staff usually accept and often seek out responsibility under the proper conditions;

- In modern industry the intellectual potential of the average person is only partly utilised.

McGregor maintained that many managers tend towards theory x and get poor results. Enlightened managers use theory y, allowing people to grow, which in turn produces better performance and results. He suggested that theory y may be difficult to put into practice in large manufacturing, shop floor operations. However, it would be more appropriate in the managing of managers and professionals.

The bottom line to McGregor's theories is: staff will contribute more to the organisation if they're treated as responsible and valued employees. Theory y, as you might gather, has replaced theory x as the dominant management philosophy in many organisations.

In the organisations I work with now, I see both theory x and theory y managers. I can think of one very large organisation in the UK who primarily have a culture of x management. They mainly employ service engineers and attempt to control them by a whole range of policies, procedures and productivity management tools. When they attend my seminars, the engineers complain about their managers and the managers complain about the engineers. I still have a lot of work to do there!

One company I've worked with issued an instruction to their sales force about a particular task they had to complete as part of their daily work. The instruction was delivered by letter from the Sales Director. It stated that this task had to be carried out, he didn't believe it was happening and anyone caught not doing it would receive a first written warning. Each sales person had to sign and return a copy of this letter.

This is theory x management. It comes from a Sales Director who doesn't believe his sales people are carrying out the task so he threatens them with dismissal. This organisation has regional managers who could have easily monitored the sales force performance on this task. The letter from the Sales Director is a further contribution to an already demotivated sales force.

I've witnessed theory x and theory y management styles and theory x is a much harder route to go. As a manager, you make life so much harder for yourself and you still don't get the results.

WHAT ABOUT YOUR MANAGER?

I hope that as you read this book you are identifying characteristics in yourself and confidently making decisions that are best for you as a Motivational Manager. But what about your manager, the person you report to – are they theory x or theory y?

Many managers that I meet on my seminars and workshops complain about their managers. They say, 'Alan, I believe what you're saying and I want to be a better Motivational Manager. However, my boss doesn't treat me in the way your proposing. He's a theory x manager.' We then go on to discuss how difficult it is to motivate your team when your manager doesn't motivate you.

There is no magic wand that will change your manager overnight. Remember – you can't make people what they're not. However, I believe that a continuous subtle education process over a period of time can produce results. Let's look at how you can deal with a theory x manager.

You may be unsure about the makeup of an x manager so here are some typical characteristics in no particular order:

- Results driven, arrogant and intolerant;

- Deadline driven;

- Detached, aloof, doesn't invite suggestions;

- Doesn't thank or praise;

- Poor listener, communicates one way;

- Issues instructions, directions, threats, never asks;

- Seeks to apportion blame;

- Doesn't delegate but think they do;

- Doesn't build teams, not concerned about morale;

- Anti-social, unhappy.

As I write this I can picture at least one manager I've worked for who displayed many of these characteristics. Do you remember I told you about the manager who tore up my report in front of me? He was that manager – typical theory x.

How do you deal with this person?

1. They are results driven so talk to them in terms of results you've achieved, what you've done, what you're going to do and when. Don't ramble on about how you're going to get there – just give them the facts and figures

2. Don't talk to them about human problems or issues in your team. They don't understand and have no interest. If anything does come up, tell them that you're dealing with it and it will be sorted. I told my 'x' manager *after* I had separated from my wife; I didn't discuss it beforehand or seek his understanding. When I told him he said, 'All I'm interested in is how it affects your ability to do your job and if it doesn't, that's fine.'

3. Always do what you say you're going to do. If you think it isn't possible, be sure of your ground and back up your reason with facts. Don't tell them what you can't do – tell them what you will do. You may have to point out that to do a certain task within a set timescale will mean that you'll be unable to allocate enough time to another task. Ask which one they want you to do.

4. Be assertive; that means not being passive or aggressive. Passivity and aggression are two natural built-in fight or flight programs that all humans have. Assertiveness is none of these; it's a learned skill and I suggest you read a book on the subject. It's about communicating your needs in a calm, clear and specific manner.

Be aware that your 'x' manager may just be a product of the culture in your organisation. Remember what I said at the start of this book; many managers learn from their managers.

If, like me, you've been managed by an 'x' manager, then you'll be aware of your level of motivation. Make sure you don't fall into the 'x' culture. I'm sure that if you're reading this book you've already made that decision; just make sure you don't become infected.

HERTZBERG'S TWO FACTOR THEORY

Frederick Hertzberg divided human needs into two categories that had a strong bearing on motivation; he called them Hygiene factors and Motivating factors. He believed that these factors were equally as important in terms of job satisfaction; however, they worked in different ways.

Hygiene, or environment, factors include:

- Salary

- Working relationships

- Working conditions

- Job security

- Style of management

- Type of work

- Working hours

According to Hertzberg, Hygiene factors don't motivate people to do their best at work. However, if they're inadequate they can be demotivating factors. In other words, they can adversely affect your job performance.

For example, if your team worked in a cold draughty office they could become seriously demotivated and they wouldn't do their jobs as well as they could. If you moved them to a warm and comfortable office it would make them happy initially but it wouldn't exactly motivate them to become consistent top performers.

I experienced something similar some years ago. The telesales team that I was responsible for were complaining about the state of their desks. How they were falling to bits and how the rough edges would catch and tear their tights. I knew that the office furniture had seen better days so I made the case to my boss to order new workstations. These were duly installed and I phoned through to the office to get the reactions. 'The team are really pleased,' said Christine. 'The new desks make such a difference.' A few weeks later I visited the site where the telesales office is located. 'What do you think of the new workstations?' I enthusiastically asked one of the team. 'Oh, I suppose they're all right,' she nonchalantly replied. I'd expected a lot more enthusiasm for all the work I'd done. However, I soon realised that the new workstations were now taken for granted and in no way would they contribute to the motivation of the team.

Another example of how the work environment could be a demotivator but not a motivator struck me one lunchtime. I was sitting in the new staff restaurant at one of my clients and was admiring the range of facilities; fabulous décor, comfortable seating areas and really bright and clean environment. There was a superb range of food on offer from a salad and a sandwich to full three-course meals. This got me thinking about my first job in the engineering factory and the lunches I used to eat there. That was like something out of a Dickens novel. Long benches and tables that everyone sat at in a soulless room; it reminded me of the dining hall at Alcatraz. I asked some of my fellow diners in this fabulous new restaurant what they thought of the facilities. 'They're okay,' shrugged a few of them. A couple of them had minor complaints but on the whole it was a feeling of complete disinterest. They accepted these facilities as a given and they certainly couldn't be regarded as a motivator. However, if you'd asked them to eat their lunch in the 'Alcatraz' dining room that I'd experienced then this would have been a huge demotivator.

These are two examples of working conditions (Hygiene factors) that could cause people to be demotivated if they were inadequate. However, they do not contribute to motivation if they are satisfactory or even excellent. If you look at the other factors that Hertzberg listed you'll understand that lack of job security could be a demotivator. However, telling a team member that they have a job for life is hardly likely to motivate them.

If a member of your team has poor working relationships then it could be a demotivator. Having good working relationships may contribute to their happiness at work but it won't be a motivating factor.

Hertzberg also listed salary as a Hygiene factor, a very controversial subject, and we're going to look at it a bit further on.

Hertzberg's Motivating factors include:

- Achievement
- Responsibility
- Recognition
- Advancement
- Challenge
- Work itself

These factors in a job are what Hertzberg suggests would encourage people to strive to do well and motivate them to do their best. Nonetheless, these factors are probably not motivators if the Hygiene factors are not satisfied.

To use my example of the telesales team, it would be hard to motivate the team members using recognition, challenge or any of the other factors if they were working in a poor environment. And of course, improving the environment alone doesn't motivate them.

MASLOW'S HIERARCHY OF NEEDS

Probably the best-known motivation theory was conceived by Abraham Maslow in the 1940s and 50s and is known as The Hierarchy of Needs. What this states is that our behaviour from moment to moment is dictated by the circumstances we find ourselves in. The lower needs have to be met before we are motivated towards higher accomplishment.

The five categories of need in the hierarchy start with Physiological and end with Self-actualisation. Let's run through the needs and then we'll come back to how they affect your job as a manager.

- **Physiological** – these are the very basic human needs such as air, water, food, sleep, sex and shelter.

- **Safety needs** – when the basic needs are more or less met, we start to think about protection from danger. We need the security of a home and possibly family in order to feel safe. We need to feel physically safe but we also need psychological safety such as job security.

- **Social or affiliation needs** – once the first two needs are satisfied, love and belonging are next on the ladder. We need social acceptance, to give and receive affection and a feeling of belonging and acceptance by others.

- **Esteem or ego needs** – there are two types of esteem needs; first is self-esteem and self-confidence. This comes from a feeling of competence, of mastering a task. Second are the respect, recognition and attention of others.

- **Self-actualisation** – at the top of the hierarchy, once all the other needs are met, is the desire to become everything that you are capable of being. Of maximising your potential to make a lasting and significant contribution.

The hierarchy is often best illustrated by the Robinson Crusoe story of a man shipwrecked on a desert island. Put yourself in Robinson's shoes (although he probably lost them in the shipwreck). Imagine crawling up the beach of the deserted island. The first thing you probably think is; 'where do I get some water? What am I going to eat?' (Physiological needs). You're hardly likely to be thinking, 'I'll build a hotel on this island and make myself a fortune!'

The next thing that goes through your mind is security. 'Are there any hostile locals on this island or wild animals who might want me for their dinner?' So, just like Robinson, you build a shelter or a stockade (Safety needs).

Once that's done you set off to explore and to your delight and excitement you find a footprint in the sand. Eventually you meet man Friday and you satisfy your need to belong and feel accepted (Social needs).

Man Friday thinks you're such a wonderful person when you show him how clever you are, share what you know and all the things you can do (Ego needs).

Once all this is in place you realise that you can't just sit about on the beach all day, you need to make something of your life. So you do all you can to get back home and become all you know you can be (Self-actualisation).

All this theory is great. However, let's translate Maslow's hierarchy into your workplace.

Say a new person joins your team. Your company gives them a salary so that they can buy food, pay the mortgage and buy clothes. So, temporarily, they are not motivated by these basic needs. Of course, this new team member is on a three-month probationary period, so although their job security is not immediately affected, they are motivated to perform well in order to continue their employment.

The new member of the team will possibly feel uncomfortable at first not knowing any of the other members. They will be motivated to become a part of the group, to be accepted by their peers. Social and affiliate needs are highly motivational for most employees until they become part of the group.

You will then find that the new person wants to do well in their job and have that recognised by the other team members.

When all of these needs have been met, the individual may start focusing on promotion; they may come after your job.

You're possibly having thoughts about one or two members of your team and realising that they don't fit the Maslow pattern. Now that could be true. However, you might find that certain members of your team are having their needs met outside the workplace.

I was chatting with one of my seminar participants over lunch one day; he appeared to be a bit of a loner in his team and not really interested in job promotion. However, he told me with much enthusiasm about his role as match secretary at his golf club. He went on at great length about all the competitions he had to organise, all the work he had to do and how important his role was in the club. I asked him if he got paid, and of course the answer was 'no.' However, I recognised that his Social and affiliation needs and his Esteem and ego needs were well satisfied in his role as match secretary. So I wouldn't dismiss Maslow or any of the other theories we've looked at. It's really important to understand or at least have a good feel for what actually motivates each of your team members.

FACTORS IN EMPLOYEE MOTIVATION

There are many other theories as to what motivates people at work. Believe me, I've studied them all. The Gallup organisation conducted research in recent years and listed Twelve Elements of Great Managing in the book *First, Break all the Rules*, published in 1999; I suggest you read it.

However, I keep coming back to research that was conducted in American industries between 1981 and 1991. I've conducted this research myself on Motivational Manager seminars and the same results keep coming up.

The purpose of the research was to identify the importance of certain factors in employee motivation and satisfaction across a range of industries.

The following ten factors describe things that people may want from their jobs. I'm sure they'll make a lot of sense to you. This is my version of them in no particular order:

- Job security

- Sympathetic understanding of personal problems

- Company loyalty to employees

- Interesting work

- Good working conditions

- Tactful discipline

- Good salary

- Growth and promotion in the organisation

- A feeling of being involved in the business

- Appreciation for work done

Managers and employees have both taken part in this research. Managers are asked to think about the members of their team and put themselves in their shoes. They are then asked to rate these factors in order of importance from 1 to 10, with 1 being the most important. I always emphasise that managers should not think in terms of what *they* consider to be the most important factors but rather what they think their team members believe. We all know that people will be motivated by different things and we all have many needs that compete to control our behaviour. However, managers are asked to 'think across the board' when considering what motivates their people.

The employees are also asked to rate these factors and the results are compared.

Employee satisfaction factors	Manager rating	Employee rating
Job security	2	4
Sympathetic understanding	9	9
Company loyalty to employees	7	8
Interesting work	5	1
Good working conditions	4	7
Tactful discipline	6	10
Good salary	1	5
Growth and promotion	3	6
A feeling of being involved	10	3
Appreciation for work done	8	2

I've conducted this research many times with managers and it always provokes lengthy and highly charged discussion. Many managers don't agree with the results from the other managers in this research, but several of them do. They also have a hard time accepting the employees' ratings. However, I believe that much of this unwillingness to accept these results comes from a lack of understanding.

Managers do tend to believe initially that money is what motivates people at work. I hear statements like:

'My people are only interested in the money.'

'That's why they come to work.'

'Sales people are motivated by money, that's why we pay them commission and bonuses.'

'You try reducing their money and see what happens.'

Many of these comments tend to come from theory x managers.

> *If you want to become a successful Motivational Manager please accept that for the majority of employees – money is not a motivator!*

However, if you want to become a successful Motivational Manager please accept that for the majority of employees – money is not a motivator!

However, as Hertzberg established in his research, if the money is not acceptable to the employee, it becomes a demotivator. If people don't feel that they're getting the correct salary then interesting work won't motivate them.

In Maslow's Hierarchy of Needs, money satisfies the basic Physiological and Safety needs; it allows us to buy food and clothing and put a roof over our head.

Yes there are people who are motivated purely by money. These are the people who work overseas or on an oil rig away from their family and friends. They work night and day, often in an inhospitable environment, just to earn money. Of course, it could be said that they're not working solely for the money, rather than what the money can buy, such as an expensive car or a large house. This in turn meets their Esteem and ego needs, winning the recognition and attention of other people.

I doubt very much that there are many well-paid employees who wake up in the morning and say, 'I must get off to my office, work really hard and give my all because I'm so well paid.'

If you increased the salary of your employees by £5000, then I'm sure they'd be really pleased and motivated to do well – but for how long? I reckon that within a couple of months that extra 5000 would be accepted as the norm with virtually no effect on motivation. And don't think it matters if it was 10,000. After a while it wouldn't make a difference.

In the survey above, managers rated job security the second most important factor in employee motivation. However, again it's a Hygiene factor. If employees felt that their job was in jeopardy then it would be a demotivator; telling them that they have a job for life is hardly going to motivate them to do better. Again it's true to say that there are a number of people who would feel motivated to do their job well because they're in a really secure job. However, the majority of employees do feel secure in their jobs and it isn't a major factor in motivation.

The managers rated promotion and growth as the third most important motivating factor. And again this is a motivator for some people. They work hard and apply themselves with the sole goal of being promoted and growing within the organisation. The majority of employees don't regard this as a motivating factor as they have either no desire to be promoted or they see it as an unattainable goal.

Let's look at what employees regard as their most important motivating factors.

Interesting work

The work itself is the most important motivating factor for the majority of employees. If they like what they do, then they're more likely to do it better. If they find their work interesting, then they will wake up in the morning wanting to get to work and make a difference.

You might be thinking, 'What if they don't like their work? How am I supposed to motivate them?' Obviously you can offset their lack of job satisfaction by taking some of the actions we've looked at earlier. Spend quality time with them, give them Confirming feedback and empower them. However, there are other practical actions you can take to make a team member's job more interesting:

- Vary the jobs they do;
- Give them more responsibility;
- Give them some of your tasks;
- Ask them to train or mentor another member of the team;
- Ask them to sit in occasionally on management meetings;
- Give them further training.

I've mentioned several times about the demotivated telesales team I inherited. Before I took over, the main task for the people in this team was to phone pubs, clubs, bars and hotels. They obtained the customer's order for different kinds of beer and entered the details into the computer system. Here are some of the actions I took to make the job more interesting for individuals and for the group:

- Christine was promoted from supervisor to team manager.

- Two members of the team were promoted to team leaders, leading a team of seven.

- A range of incentives, product promotions and team competitions were introduced.

- Each member of the team spent time with a field sales person visiting customers.

- Product knowledge sessions were conducted to give the team a better understanding of the different beers sold by the company.

- New products were introduced, including soft drinks, wine and spirits.

- Everyone attended a wine appreciation seminar.

- Friday afternoons were designated as party times (with the work still getting done).

- The team became involved in fundraising activities and charity events.

- The team took part in a national telesales competition (they came second).

Many other things took place with the objective of making the job more interesting – of making it fun!

This is probably a totally different business from the one you work in but I'm sure you could produce your own list that would make your team members' jobs more interesting and much more fun.

Nobody motivates today's workers. If it doesn't come from within, it doesn't come. Fun helps remove the barriers that allow people to motivate themselves.

Herman Cain (American businessman, founder of
Godfather Pizza)

Appreciation

The second most important motivation factor that employees rated was appreciation for work done.

This brings us back to Confirming feedback; employees want to be told when they've done something well. Let's face it, everyone wants to know when they've done well; children, teenagers and your nearest and dearest.

In the workplace, it's not about telling people once a year or every six months at their formal appraisal; it's about doing it every time you experience a member of your team doing something well.

Remember what we said earlier: 'You get more of what you reward.' If you reward a team member with some Confirming feedback, they will be highly motivated to do the same thing again and do it better. There are also practical things you can do to show appreciation:

- The occasional gift

- Time off work

- Gift vouchers

- Personal thank you letters

- A mention in the company newsletter or magazine

- Attend corporate events

Some of the things I used to do for my telesales team:

- Took cakes or doughnuts when I visited the team.

- Organised a letter from the Chief Executive when an individual or the team had performed well.

- Sent members of the team on any corporate events that were organised for customers.

- Organised a scheme where people could win gift vouchers based on individual and team performance.

- Delivered flowers on a birthday or any other important day.

- Seasonal celebration days such as Christmas or Easter.

I'm sure you could come up with many more tangible things you could do to say 'thank you' to your team. However, a few words of warning; never use any incentive or gift as a replacement for Confirming feedback. A genuine word of thanks delivered in the correct way is worth far more in terms of motivation then any tangible gift or bonus.

> *A genuine word of thanks delivered in the correct way is worth far more in terms of motivation then any tangible gift or bonus.*

A feeling of being in on things

The third factor that employees rated as important in motivation was a feeling of being in on things, of being involved in the business. Employees want to know that what they do has an influence on the success of the team and the business. They will be highly motivated if they understand that they are actually making a difference.

> *Employees want to know that what they do has an influence on the success of the team and the business.*

Employees also want to be asked their opinion; they realise that you may not always be able to implement what they suggest but they will feel valued if you ask and consider what they say.

That's why it's so important to spend quality time with each member of your team; we looked at this in Chapter 3. It gives you an excellent opportunity to get feedback from each person. It allows you to tell them how the team is performing within the organisation and how they contribute to organisation as a whole.

Here are some practical things you can do to satisfy a team member's need to feel in on things:

- Let them attend meetings.

- Give them all the information and let them run a briefing meeting.

- Ask for opinions.

- Report back on their feedback to you.

Some of the actions I used to take with my team:

- They all attended a weekly briefing meeting.

- They attended monthly sales meetings with the field sales team.

- They attended the national sales conference.

- They attended meetings with the technical engineers.

- They were encouraged to suggest how we might better serve our customers.

- They were consulted on how best to run a product promotion.

Again I'm sure you could come up with many ideas that would be relevant to your business.

Hire the best. Pay them fairly. Communicate frequently. Provide challenges and rewards. Believe in them. Get out of their way and they'll knock your socks off.

Mary Ann Allison (American author)

SUMMING UP

All of the motivation theories we've looked at have their flaws and detractors. However, they do give you some guidelines as to how you can create a motivational environment for your people. Your team members will be motivated by different factors and that's why it's so important to spend quality time with them and to get to know them. You need to understand your team members from a business point of view and a human point of view.

If you have a team member who's going through personal problems outside the workplace, then they're unlikely to be motivated at work by any of the factors we've just looked at. In Maslow's Hierarchy of Needs their Security needs must be satisfied before they can move on to anything else.

You must also remember that the members of your team are not robots, they are complex human beings. That's why I said right at the start of this book that the job of the Motivational Manager can be difficult. These humans all see the world in a different way. You may be motivated by a specific factor but they may not. You may be motivated to develop and grow in the organisation but they may just want to enjoy their job and be appreciated for what they do.

Ironically, the factors that managers rated highly as motivators are often hard to achieve. It's probably extremely difficult for you to increase a team member's salary. I'm also sure that you can't do much about their job security. And you certainly can't ensure that they all get promoted and grow in the organisation.

What you can do much more easily and at very little or no cost is:

- Make their job more interesting by giving them some new tasks;

- Give them feedback and appreciation for what they do;

- Make them feel in on things by Power Listening and speaking with them on a regular basis.

As I've said before, I've done this job; I'm not a social psychologist or an academic. I know how tough it is and I appreciate the challenges you face.

I've used all techniques we've looked at in this book. They worked very successfully for me and I know they will work for you.

I wish you every success.

Index

Need a Dynamic Speaker?

Alan Fairweather has been motivating and inspiring audiences from around the world for the past thirteen years. Alan's seminars and speeches are entertaining, inspirational and thought provoking. He is very much results driven and is committed to helping participants in a practical way. He creates a non-threatening environment that generates fun and encourages people to learn.

Schedule Alan for your next conference or meeting – CONTACT:

Alan Fairweather International

6 Keith Row

Edinburgh EH4 3NL

Scotland UK

Tel: +44(0) 131 315 2687

Email: alan@themotivationdoctor.com

Website: www.themotivationdoctor.com

JOIN THE MASTER MOTIVATORS CLUB

Visit Alan's website and subscribe to the Master Motivators Club. Each month you will receive a free email newsletter with tips, techniques, skills and strategies for building business. Discover how to motivate your team, motivate your customers and motivate yourself.